The Book of
PAIGNTON

The Town and Its People

December 17th 2001.

Dear Mike,

Wishing you a "Very Happy Birthday."
Hope this will bring back many happy
memories.

All my love

Betty
xxx

The Book of
PAIGNTON

The Town and Its People

FRANK PEARCE

HALSGROVE

First published in Great Britain in 2001

*Dedicated to my wife Joan for all her
practical support, patience and encouragement.*

Frontispiece photograph: *Victoria Street in
the early 1900s as seen from Station Square.*

British Library Cataloguing-in-Publication Data
A CIP record for this title is available from the British Library

ISBN 1 84114 113 5

HALSGROVE
PUBLISHING, MEDIA AND DISTRIBUTION

Halsgrove House
Lower Moor Way
Tiverton, Devon EX16 6SS
Tel: 01884 243242
Fax: 01884 243325
email: sales@halsgrove.com
website: http://www.halsgrove.com

Printed and bound in Great Britain by Bookcraft Ltd., Midsomer Norton.

*Whilst every care has been taken to ensure the accuracy of the
information contained in this book, the author disclaims responsibility
for any mistakes which may have inadvertently been included.*

FOREWORD

The Book of Paignton, with its many photographs and literary recollections, has been compiled as an evocative record of the resort since Victoria's reign. The last 100 years is an ocean upon which we have all sailed, and here we remember its capricious moods, its storms and calms, the pleasures along the way and those in whose company we travelled. Through these and other memories the facts of our history unfold.

So often the mists of time veil realism so that substance melts into shadow and consequently we use our imagination to conceive pictures of the past as we would wish them to be rather than as they were. But as we grow older these beacons of light though now dim and flickering provide a glow of comfort to ailing memory for we often resurrect the good things, inter the bad and in doing so, find consolation, however transitory. Contemporary and past history make strange bedfellows for they each accuse the other of failures and follies. However critical we may be of other transient periods it is hard not to admit that the ingredients of today's life of violence and vandalism are in danger of replacing former rectitude and temperance.

Frank Pearce
AD2001

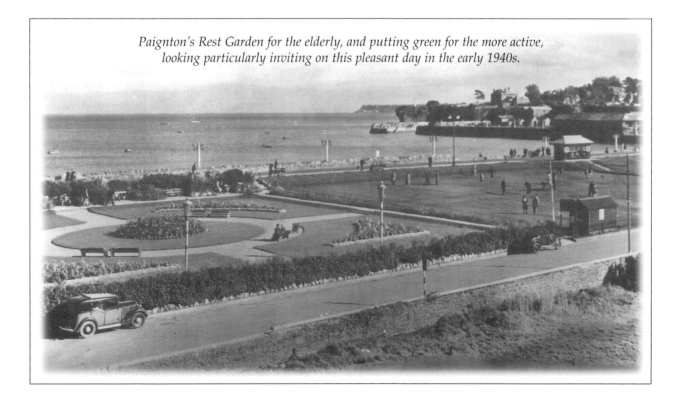

Paignton's Rest Garden for the elderly, and putting green for the more active,
looking particularly inviting on this pleasant day in the early 1940s.

Kirkham House is one of Paignton's oldest historic buildings and is believed to have its origins in the 14th or 15th century. Kirkham House has close affiliation with Paignton's Bishop's Palace and despite the obscurity of its genealogy it is now accepted as an important part of English history.

Kirkham Cottages.

PREFACE

It is a great pleasure to write a foreword for Frank Pearce's excellent pictorial book on Paignton, having lived here for most of my life since 1910 apart from the war years, and studying and practising in London in the 1930s. So I have many memories through the years which I still recall well. The book's many splendid photographs show how the town has developed.

Historically Paignton is the oldest of the three bay towns. Its history dates back to Saxon times in the 7th century AD when it was predominantly a farming community. The Saxons built a church and the Coverdale Tower, the latter being associated with St Boniface who was born in Crediton in AD680. He also became the Saint of the City of Dokkum in Friesland, Holland. By an amazing coincidence Rotary International twinned the Paignton and Dokkum Clubs in the 1950s. In the Domesday Book Paignton is recorded as Peintona and as having 20 hides with 52 villeins, 40 bordars and 36 serfs and their families.

The earliest part of the town centred around Winner Street, Church Street and Well Street, and much of the land toward the sea was marshland. As this land was reclaimed and the town grew, Palace Avenue, then Victoria Street, and later Torbay Road became the three main shopping streets. The Green was given to the people of Paignton for all time to be kept as it was, and although this has not happened it remains an enormous asset to the town.

The railway was built during the 1860s and the Great Western Railway developed the safest signalling system in the whole country. During the first 40 years of the 20th century its trains brought thousands of visitors to the town every summer, and the famous King and Castle were the finest examples of steam engines. The Torbay Limited ran daily to Paddington in three hours and 54 minutes stopping only at Torquay on the way. All trains were so regular that the time could be told by their departures and arrivals!

In the early 1900s a tramway linked Paignton and Torquay, and extended all over Torquay. The fares from Waycotts Corner in Hyde Road to Seaway Road were 1d., to Torquay station 2d., and 3d. to the Strand in Torquay. Later they were replaced by Devon General buses.

Perhaps the most famous building in the town is Oldway Mansion, now the Council Offices. Originally completed for Isaac Singer in 1875 it was completely remodelled in 1904 by Paris Singer to its present style. During the First World War it became a hospital for wounded soldiers, and was requisitioned for the duration of the Second World War by the RAF which had an Initial Training Wing for aircrew there. During this war Paignton, like all the bay and nearby coastal towns, was bombed by German hit-and-run raiders. The bombs were dropped before the sirens could sound, so there was no chance of taking shelter. Fortunately Paignton escaped more lightly than the others and suffered fewer casualties.

As the lower town grew, the first main shops in Torbay Road were on the north side, then Queens Park Mansions and the shops below were built with Dellers Grocery, the chemist's shop and toy shops,

Coverdale Tower or, more correctly, 'The Bishop's Tower'.

and Dellers Café on the south side. My father came to Paignton in 1910 to open the chemist's shop, and after the First World War he qualified as an optician and started the practice which today still bears his name in Hyde Road. Below Queens Road all the houses were private ones, but as tourism developed, Queens Road, Sands Road, Adelphi Road, Garfield Road, and Kernou and Beach Roads became mostly hotels and guest-houses, while lower Torbay Road converted to shops and cafés. The splendid buildings in Esplanade Road – at first all private houses – became hotels in due course. The larger Singer building, now the Palace Hotel, was enclosed in a 10ft red-brick wall from the Esplanade Hotel, now the Inn on the Green, as far as Polsham Road. The Redcliffe Hotel with its outstanding position was built as a private residence for Col Robert Smith and completed in 1865. It was bought by Paris Singer in 1877, and sold in 1902 when it became the hotel.

Some of my early recollections are of the bathing machines on the beach at the bottom of Torbay Road, and the double row of canvas tents on the beach north of the pier – my family had one of these for a number of years. I also recall Pelosi's and Valley's horse- and hand-drawn ice-cream carts plying up and down the sea front in the summer, with penny cornets and twopenny and threepenny wafers, and later Dimeo's as well. At Pelosi's chip cart in Station Square in the winter we could buy twopennyworth of tasty chips fried in 'best hotel dripping'. I remember Paignton Rovers playing football on the Green and also the disaster of the pavilion on the pier being destroyed by fire in 1919 (to remain derelict for many years, but now at last beginning to look more worthy of the town once again).

One of my earliest memories was of the first troops to be billeted in Paignton at the beginning of the First World War. They were the Post Office Rifles and several of them often visited us bringing sweets which made them very popular. After their training was finished other Regiments followed, among them the RAMC. After the war two German destroyers which were being towed to be destroyed broke loose from their tows and were wrecked, one on Preston Beach and the other off Roundham Head, where they remained for some years before being removed.

A novel entertainment after the war was the Avro aeroplane which gave trips from the north side of the Green, at five shillings for a trip around the bay, or £1 or more for longer trips including looping the loop. When the average child's pocket-money was 1s.6d. a week – this was very expensive. Later, seaplanes took over as a less risky option for the public. We also had the annual Anderton and Rowlands Fair with its roundabouts, swings, helter-skelter, cakewalk, stalls and sideshows. The famous Golden Dragons came later as did the dodgem cars. The traction engines and the colourful caravans have long since been replaced by modern caravans and trailers, and the amusements grow ever more sophisticated.

While Paignton does not have the historical events that Brixham boasts, we have had our share of international sportsmen and women. In rugby we had the Woodgate twins, and Richard Sharp, a Montpelier schoolboy who played for England. In cricket Dickie Bird was a Paignton Club professional before becoming a world-famous umpire, and he scored a number of centuries in Queens Park. In tennis we had Sue Barker as one of England's leading players, later to become a BBC sports commentator and presenter.

I hope that these few reminiscences serve to provide a suitable entry for Frank's book and that it will be enjoyed to the same extent as were his previous volumes.

Philip Baker

CONTENTS

*This aerial photo gives a splendid view of the relative distance between
Goodrington, Roundham Head, Young's Park and Paignton Sands and Pier.*

*Looking across Paignton from Redburn Road showing the
Gas Works, church and the Corn Mill in Littlegate Road.*

ACKNOWLEDGEMENTS

I have many kind people to thank who have loaned documents, treasured records or scrapbooks or who have given special information on Paignton's history. My sincere gratitude to Philip Baker who has been kind enough to draw on his experience of Paignton's past to write a rewarding and comprehensive preface.

A grateful thank you to David Mason, Ivan Martin and John Mann who have been a tower of strength in loaning priceless photographs of the town's bygone days. There have been so many kind people who have contributed in a variety of ways, among whom are Max Danby of Flair Photography, Graham and June Headon, Terry Clifford, Michael Adams, Peggy and David Head, Arthur Day, Donald Wood, Roy Ward, Mrs Patterson and Deidre Wood. My unreserved appreciation to Tony Moss, Ron and Pamela Fenton, Harry Truscott and Betty Tuckett. I have been most fortunate in having the support of Hayes Road School (Mrs Morgan) and Collaton School (Mr Mantel).

My thanks also to all those who have given liberally of their time in furthering the production of this book, including Nick Pannell of the *Herald Express*, Christine Lambert of Paignton Zoo, Chris and Linda Roach, Brian Carter, Terry Kerryson, Derek Webber, Jill Farrant, Derek Pearce, Jack Baker, Sue Cox, Doris Wills, Pru Pearse, Doll King and Lorna Gardner.

And finally a thank you to the *Herald Express* for permission to use their photographs of the D-Day celebrations.

These old cottages at the southern end of Paignton's sea front were demolished in 1882 to make way for the building of the Paignton Club House. The spacious land beyond the cottages is now Cleveland Road.

This unusual picture is of a pumping machine in Victoria Park pumping water to the site where now stands the Palace Hotel (formerly another of Isaac Singer's residences).

A very early photograph of an undeveloped Broad Sands shows practically no houses in the area and the stretch of land of the distant hills still undeveloped.

INTRODUCTION

The resort of Paignton lodged on the English Riviera and situated almost midway between Torquay and Brixham is acknowledged as one of the most popular and leading holiday haunts in the British Isles.

The advent of the Industrial Revolution in Great Britain in the late-18th century brought enterprising entrepreneurs and eminent scientists a period of opportunity and discovery which transformed British society. The lives of millions of people in the middle ground of industrial England were radically changed, mostly for the better, lifting them from the squalid conditions and vagaries of land cultivation to the awakening of new horizons. It was the renaissance that brought George and Robert Stephenson the loco-motive 'Rocket', steam power and eventually the railway. And it was from this latter that Paignton's popularity as a seaside resort grew and prospered.

Prior to Queen Victoria's death in 1901, Paignton existed in a spirit of comparative calm. The cabbie and his faithful horse were the accepted means of trans-port, the clippity-clop of hooves the only sound disturbing the peace of its streets. But with the turn of the century the resort awakened to the new challenge of invention and technological advancement. Henry Ford's cars, the Wright Brothers' conquest of the skies and Marconi's wireless were all radical changes in the normal pattern of life, and this time marked also a scientific revolution.

With such a surge of development and prosperity, new opportunities presented themselves, among them the prospect of a holiday by the sea, an experience hith-erto denied to most. In keeping with other seaside towns along the South Coast, Paignton Council, prompted by their committees, launched extensive advertising campaigns in the Midlands and elsewhere promoting Paignton as a family holiday destination.

The response was overwhelming. During the holiday season, trainloads of visitors were arriving in Paignton at weekends at almost hourly intervals. Subsequently, Paignton's population would often increase by many as 25000, placing a severe strain on water supplies and other services. Hotels and guest-houses were filled to capacity; 'No Vacancies' signs legion. At these times it was not unusual to see people sleeping on the beaches overnight. Such was the demand for beds that the Council issued appeals to private houses to co-operate by letting spare bedrooms.

Paignton responded whole-heartedly, and although the practice of letting garden sheds was officially forbidden, they were sometimes surrepti-tiously brought into service to meet demand. Thankfully during these emergencies, HM Inspectors of Health and Safety appear to have suffered from severe myopia for no summonses were ever recorded. Fortunate also was the fact that during that period Paignton's weather pattern was superb and through the day its extensive sands and promenades with its wide green sward thronged with people.

As a resident of Paignton, the writer recalls what little rain fell during those crowded summers; a time when the Ministry of Sunshine smiled benevolently on Paignton and its beaches. On most days, a galaxy of colour laced the sea strands with a chromatic pageantry of swimsuits, the air filled with the sound of gurgling sea waves and a multiplicity of chatter mingling with children's screams of delight – no less than was the case at nearby Preston and Goodrington Sands where the gently shelving beaches were often crowded.

In Paignton, as a result of the shortage of holiday accommodation, hundreds of private houses were permanently converted into small hotels and guest-houses. Ostentatious sign boards appeared in every colour, shape and size, adorning streets and roads like bannered corridors, each declaring offers of the latest mod-cons.

Times Past
by Frank Pearce

Time future speeds towards us in his own relentless way
And in the passing plants the kiss of instant time
And then without delay
Is gone, becomes time past and never will return.

Time walks with kings and beggar men alike,
And shows no deference to the one or pity to the other,
For each must serve in his own way, none may escape the call,
For time the master of itself is master of us all.

Wealth cannot check his onward march with gifts of paltry gold,
For time, unloved and loving not, impassionate and cold,
Moves on, without a glance, to know how mankind fares
Or let poverty delay his step with postulated prayers.

Left: *Shorton Lane, leading to Sleepy Lane. Sleepy Lane still exists much as it was 100 years ago, having remained undisturbed and unspoilt by the march of avaricious development.*

A few of the staff of the well-known building firm of Lewis's who played their part in the development of Paignton. Left to right: Bill Lay, ?, Rod Cose, Stan Alfrod, Ken Lewis.

These old cottages in Southfield Road were demolished in the 1950s to allow for road widening.

CHAPTER 1

STREET SCENES

CHURCH STREET & AROUND

Records show that as far back as 1295, during the reign of Edward I, a weekly market and a yearly fair were held in Church Street on 'the vigil, fast and morrow of the Holy Trinity'. It is of special interest, for this market was established 525 years before the first public market in Torquay. Dating from Elizabeth I's reign in 1567, the Pembroke Survey reveals that beer apparently played an important part in daily life, for there were three 'Heywards' (collectors of taxes) and also four 'Ale tasters'. Of the latter the Survey says: 'they do present all brewenges and typlings' and indeed it was the ale taster's responsibility to sample and advise on the quality of beverages. The four referred to in the Survey were at Paignton, Pruston (Preston), Yalbourne (Yalberton) and Blackdon (Blagdon), and there were also other such personages at Stoke and Marledon (Marldon).

The life and business of Paignton centred around Church Street, the Parish Church of St John the Baptist and the two inns (the Victoria and the

This photograph of Church Street was taken around the mid 1920s. The Pook family owned the butchery business which was later taken over by the Hoopers. At that time the Pooks owned large stretches of farmland in an area from Tweenaway to Churston. The horse and trap are standing outside Crown and Anchor Way, with the next shop on that side being Western's Bakers and Confectioners. Next door was Heads' Milk and Dairy Produce adjoining a cottage next to the London Inn. It was here in 1934 that a great fire almost destroyed the property. Fortunately the shops opposite were in no danger for the wind carried the flames in the opposite direction. The Coysh family owned some of these shops on that side including the Church Street Post Office. Some elderly Paigntonians may also remember Mrs Martin's drapery, Mr Stoneman's fruit and veg shop, Brown's the Herbalist and other little retailers who stocked a multiplicity of items from saucers to saucepans, dummies to doorknobs.

Coach House, formerly the London Inn) plus 15 shops. The Parish Church is the fourth church to have been built on the site and foundations under the floor suggest that a house of worship stood there as far back as the Saxon age.

More correctly 'The Bishop's Tower', Coverdale Tower was part of the massive fortifications built to protect the Palace of Osbern and the resident Bishop of Exeter. The tower itself is 14th or 15th century in origin and was built as part of the coastal sea defence. For many years it has been popularly known as 'Coverdale Tower' based on the belief that Miles Coverdale worked there on his famous translation of the Bible. But this is incorrect for Coverdale did not come to Devon until 16 years after his translation had been published.

The great room above Crown and Anchor Way in Church Street was at one time used as the Magistrate's courthouse and a business centre for the town where the newly formed Local Board of Health held their first meeting in September 1863. By the early 1900s the property had been divided into two, halving the size of the former courtroom. Crown and Anchor Way was also used as a staging post for the London stage-coach where, in the spacious yard beyond, tired horses could be exchanged for fresh ones.

When the days of the staging post ended, the yard became a slaughterhouse and as late as the early 1900s elderly people can remember herds of cattle and sheep being driven down through adjacent Well Street into Church Street, charging against the shop fronts and on through the archway into the yard.

Church Street's quaint little shops created a market ambience with locals from the surrounding catchment eager to discover a bargain.

CHURCH STREET SHOPS IN THE EARLY 1900s

W.H. Western	Bakers (small loaf 3d., large 4d.)
W. Hooper	Butchers
R. Miniffi	Sweets (chocolate bars 2d., sherbet ½d.)
B. Ashplant	Electrician
J. Barker	Fish and chips
D. Head	Dairy and ice-cream (wafers and cornets 2d.)
S. Isaacs Barber	(haircut 4d.)
M. Battershaw	Footwear (boots 10s.0d.)
C. Brown	Apothecary
W. Stoneman	Fruit and veg (large Jaffa oranges 2d.)
W. Coysh	Post Office and stationery
D. Martin	Haberdashery
S. Evans	Gent's outfitter (suits £3, hats 3s.9d.)
J. Osborne	Tailor
F. Carter	Toys

This is Well Street leading up to Church Street. The water from here supplied the whole community in the area. As early as 1863, the well was piped off to supply other communities. The people of Well Street, like the man holding the bucket, had to fetch their water from a gushing stream behind and to the man's left. The door in the wall immediately behind him led to the milking yard. From before the early 1900s it was through this street that large herds of cattle were driven to reach the slaughter yard at the rear of Crown and Anchor Way.

Church Street was a very busy shopping centre where many of the nearby streets converged. Fêtes, market days and local and national celebrations were almost always held in Church Street. Here the 1935 Silver Jubilee celebrations are in progress. There appear to be almost 100 women in the procession so this photograph perhaps depicts a group such as the Mothers' Union taking part in the celebrations. Clearly visible on the left is Heads' Dairy next to Western's Bakers and Confectioners. Next is Crown and Anchor Way and the shop beyond is Hoopers' Butchers while opposite is Coysh's Post Office. Note the flag at the top of the street, on which the town's name is spelt the old way – Paynton.

Palace Avenue at the turn of the century. The lady with the white parasol seems to be greatly interested in what appears to be a penny-farthing bicycle. On the left is Lloyd's Bank and on the far right Deller's Supply Stores, now Rossiters.

❧ A.E. DEY ❧

A.E. Dey, Grocer and Provision Dealer, was sited at the end of Church Street and had a very prosperous and efficient business. In the 1920s, horses and carts would trundle their way past the shop towards Hyde Road and the town centre.

By the 1930s, Deys were the proud owners of this Wolseley trader van. The company's smart vehicles became a familiar sight among the town's business traffic.

ை THE PARISH CHURCH ை

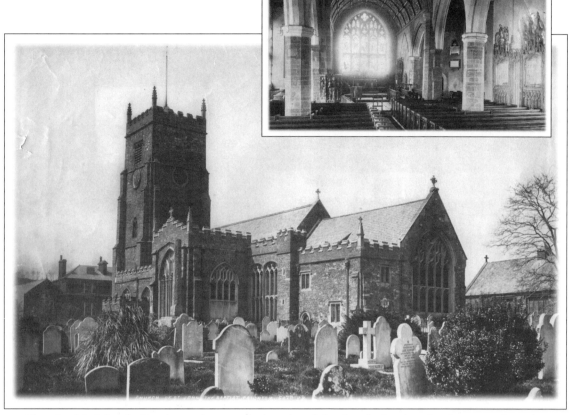

Church of St John the Baptist, and inset; *the interior of the church showing the chantry and reredos.*

The morning service in Paignton's Parish Church is over and the vicar's flock seek pastures green.

ᔥ THE PARISH CHURCH ᔥ

A special service at Paignton Parish Church. The clergy conduct a procession at the induction of the new Vicar of Paignton Parish Church with Marldon, the Reverend Reval Giles MA on 12 February 1909.

Left: *The gruesome aspects of war are all too plainly shown here on the walls of the Parish Church of Paignton where bowmen's arrow heads were sharpened ready for battle. Here also stood the Crown and Anchor Inn. The building was demolished in 1892 and replaced by an archway called Crown and Anchor Way leading to Palace Avenue.*

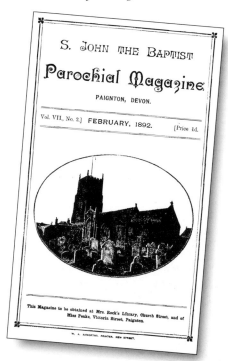

This was the Parish Church Magazine cover issued by the Church of St John the Baptist, in Church Street, 1892. Price – 1d.

❧ BUSINESS & COMMERCE ❧

An extract from Billings Directory and Gazetteer of Devon *1857 reads: 'Paignton has long been noted for its cider and cabbages; the cabbages have obtained a widespread name (Paignton Cabbages) and grow very large and far surpass every other sort; great quantities of them are annually sent off to all the neighbouring towns.' This rare photograph is of the cabbage-growing grounds before Queen's Park was developed, c.1870, overlooking Palace Avenue.*

Right: The farm's water supply was obtained from this little stream nearby. Tall pipes to road level height facilitated easy delivery.

Left: This is the entrance to The Linhay, an insemination farm in Grange Road which existed as far back as the 1940s.

❧ BUSINESS & COMMERCE ☙

ARTHUR WAYCOTT,
Wine ⁕ and ⁕ Spirit ⁕ Merchant,
WINNER STREET, PAIGNTON.

Lipton's and Maypole's were two of the most popular grocery stores in the town, both being household names in the 1920s. Situated as they were in the main street they captured most of the general trade.

ᥴᥴ BUSINESS & COMMERCE ᥴᥴ

Suttons during the 1930s. Left to right, back: P. Thomas, H. Hurrell, L. Johnson, W. Gaisford, H. Young, M. Rippingale; middle: *M.A. Sutton, J. Sutton, M.J. Sutton, J. Sutton, M. Brewster;* front: *J. McVicar, A. Woolacott, I. Baker. Suttons Printers will be remembered by older Paigntonians as an intrinsic part of Paignton's business and social life. The late Mr and Mrs Sutton opened their first shop in November 1906 at Number 2 Garfield Terrace, now known as 63 Torbay Road. Just before the First World War they again moved further down Torbay Road where the family business continued until 1960 when Miss Margaret Sutton, well known for her long association with the musical life of the town, retired, and the premises were sold and reconstructed as Mario's Ice Cream Parlour.*

William Hicks' Dairy & Poultry Shop enjoyed a prime position in Palace Avenue. It is pictured here in October 1914, a few weeks after the outbreak of the First World War.

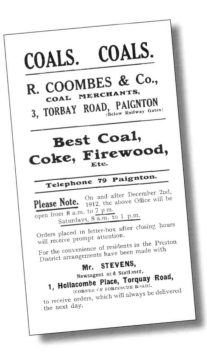

BUSINESS & COMMERCE

PRINTING AND BOOKBINDING

OF EVERY DESCRIPTION
Promptly and Cheaply executed.

Invitations, Programmes, Visiting Cards, Memorial Cards, &c., on the shortest notice.

W. A. AXWORTHY, Torbay Printing Works,
NEW STREET, PAIGNTON.

J. W. DAW,
10 & 11, VICTORIA STREET,
PAIGNTON,
Fancy and General Draper,
Costumier.
Mantle Maker, Milliner, &c.

Agent for Dr. Jaeger's all wool Clothing and Bedding.

W. MERSON,
Chemist and Mechanical Dentist, Paignton.
PRESCRIPTIONS PREPARED.

H. MARLEY,
General Draper, Hosier, Outfitter, &c.
PAIGNTON.

Family and Furnishing Drapery, Linens, Carpets, Dress and Mantle Materials.

FURS, MANTLES, MILLINERY, LACE, HOSIERY, GLOVES, RIBBONS, WOOLS, HABERDASHERY, &c.

Separate Shop adjoining for Gentlemen's and Juveniles' Ready-made Clothing, Tailoring and General Outfitting.

CLOSE AT 2 ON WEDNESDAYS.   TERMS—CASH.

T. LUTLEY,
Palace Avenue Dairy, Paignton.

NEW MILK DELIVERED TWICE DAILY, 3½d. PER QUART.

POULTRY, FRUIT, &c.

PALK & SONS, BUTCHERS.

ESTABLISHED 1827.

Winner Street and Victoria Street, Paignton (Telephone 101)
18 Lower Union Street, Torquay (Telephone 38).

Experienced Men sent to take and execute orders daily.

꿍 COLLEY END ROAD 㣩

Here at the bottom of Colley End Road on the junction where Well Street, Kirkham Street and Cecil Road are contiguous, there once stood a large drinking fountain for cattle and horses. Mr Michael Adams recalls how on hot summer days, thirsty cattle en route to the slaughter yard at the rear of Crown and Anchor Way would sometimes stampede down the hill to reach the welcoming water-filled fountain. It became a source of delight and fair game for the children of the nearby RC Elementary School – seen opposite here in the last-known picture of the school before demolition – who would throw considerable quantities of stones and rubbish into the trough. The efforts of the Council staff to keep it clean proved of little avail for as fast as it was cleared it became the object of another refill. On this site and prior to the fountain years there stood a barn from which old Paigntonians will remember the name Barn Hill.

Perhaps these two little girls (now grown up) will remember the Colley End fountain.

ഛ WINNER STREET ഇ

Winner Street, 1908. There is a delivery cart outside Eastman's (Company Shop) butchers. The tall man holding the horse's reins has a traditional gold Albert watch and chain which shows clearly against his Edwardian waistcoat. The two gas lamps are of interest. A ten-year agreement with the Gas Co. had been sealed in 1905 and as a result 200 new lanterns and incandescent burners were provided leaving only a very few flat-flame burners in operation. It wasn't until January 1909 that the first public electric street lamps were in position. The footwear shop opposite Eastmans could well be the first Paignton Co-operative shop. It appears to be on the same site where Plymco stands today.

*An unusual scene of Winner Street in 1900 when a heavy
snow fall turned every street into a Christmas picture.*

∽ WINNER STREET ∽

A century-old photograph of Clase's Tea Rooms in Winner Street, not far from adjoining Church Street. This was a popular meeting place for the locals.

One of the oldest photographs in the book, this shows members of the Winner Street Baptist Church outside the church in 1890. The Pastor at this time was the Revd W. Price.

⌘ VICTORIA STREET ⌘

Station Square in the early 1900s. The motor cars equal the number of horses here, a sign that the days of cabbies were numbered. On the right is the Gerston Hotel where the first showing of Gilbert & Sullivan's Pirates of Penzance *took place. The tall lamppost and kiosk (centre) have long since gone.*

The view from Station Square looking towards Victoria Street. A Great Western Railway bus awaits passengers for its service to Totnes, c.1905. The lady with her infant in the pram crossing the road at this point would stand little chance of survival these days.

ശ TORQUAY ROAD ଡ

Torquay Road in 1915 in the era of the tram approaching the junction with Seaway Road.

*Torquay Road in 1950 showing the same junction with Seaway Road
before the Preston traffic lights and one-way system were introduced.*

ↀ TORBAY ROAD ↀ

Torbay Road from an early postcard.

Shopping Week, 1920. This was one of Paignton Chamber of Commerce's organised yearly 'Shopping Week' efforts. There were competitions for the best-dressed windows and other attractions designed to stimulate trade. That they were successful is evidenced by these crowds in Torbay Road. Such attendance was typical of many other events including regattas and carnivals.

TORBAY ROAD

Torbay Road from another early postcard.

The lake in Victoria Park. Originally this was marshland where water accumulated from several higher sources. Although it provided a supply for many nearby properties it was also used as a sewer. Paignton's first Local Board of Health was set up in 1863, meeting at the Crown and Anchor Inn, Church Street. From the records over the next ten years, the business of every meeting concentrated on the appalling sewage conditions in the town and the imminent danger of disease and fever. Despite all the efforts of the Local Board to clean up the place, the coming of the railway 1859 and the laying of gas mains 1860, there was much dissension between the 'let us bide as us be' inhabitants and the moderns.

ᏬᎿ INNS ᏬᎾ

*The Old Manor House Inn in Old Torquay Road is one of the oldest
in the South West of England and dates back to the 16th century.*

*The Torbay Inn in Fisher Street dates back to 1649. The street is sometimes spelt Fischer
Street, having been referred to in that form on the 1567 survey where Winner Street is
Wynderde Street (Vineyard Street) pointing to a medieval wine industry with the present
Torbay Inn adjacent. This picture of the inn was taken in 1932 with some of the patrons
setting off on a trip to Dartmoor. Among those in the picture whose names have been traced
are Fred Pottinger, Tom Cole, Ed Pottinger, Bill King, Edward King and Olga King
(née Pritchard).*

⁓⁓ STENTIFORD'S CORNER ⁓⁓

This was always known as Stentiford's Corner (the newsagency) but is now known as Hyde Road Corner. When the trams ceased in 1934 the shop was demolished and rebuilt 15 feet to the right. The notice reads 'Last chance to win Derby £1000' – perhaps it was also a betting shop?

This picture shows the early trams in Paignton in 1910. This one is turning from the Torquay Road into Hyde Road at Stentiford's Corner with what appears to be a full load of passengers.

∽ TRAMS ∽

An early excursion from the time trams first started to appear in the area, c.1907.
Note the curtained windows.

The tram at the terminus in Hyde Road awaits its return to Torquay. At the end of the trolley arm, on the top deck, is a grooved wheel fitted on to the overhead electrified cable to feed power to the tram. The driver could transfer his brass driving levers to either end of the vehicle. The triple wooden bars just above the tram lines were nick-named cow-catchers to prevent any pedestrians being drawn under. The name originated from the big American trains which travelled the prairies across cattle country.

⇢ THE MOTOR CAR & CHARABANCS ⇣

Palace Avenue on a quiet morning in the primitive days of the motor car. The vehicle passing Lloyds Bank looks remarkably like a Bugatti Landaulette, a classic car in those days. Rossiters now stands where Deller's Supply Stores are shown in the photograph.

A 30-seater correctly filled to its capacity ready to take off on a day's Mothers' Union outing in one of the Redcliffe's Cars charabancs during the mid 1920s.

☙ THE MOTOR CAR & CHARABANCS ☚

This 30-seater charabanc with 36 passengers aboard appears to be on its way to Paignton or Torquay from Brixham. Its solid tyres, bulb-press horn and oil lamps date it to c.1914.

Passengers in Oliver and Curtis's coach set off for a day trip in 1924.
Note the speed limit sign on the side of the bus - 12 mph.

෧ THE GWR ෨

The broad-gauge rail track in 1866 from Torre to Paignton. Here, the track skirts the Hollacombe Gas Works. It has long since been demolished.

The Great Western Railway proudly shows off one of its road transporters in 1905 outside the Gerston Hotel in Station Square. It had a roof but this provided very little protection in driving rain. In the background can be seen the old railway footbridge.

Distant view of Broadsands at Elbury with I.K. Brunel's viaduct standing as a lasting memorial to the great man.

⋈ THE GWR ⋈

The Gerston Royal Hotel and Station Square at the turn of the century with the driver of some sort of mechanical transport awaiting fares.

The railway at Preston with Preston Sands in the background.

A Great Western Railway omnibus and two unusual passenger transporters with solid tyres discharge their parties on the seaward side of Paignton Green on a misty day in 1914.

CHAPTER 2

THE PLEASURE RESORT

The Esplanade Hotel was built by Hyde Dendy around 1885. It was originally two large villas which he joined together before adding the tower and a dormitory block. Behind the building a cycle track was laid out, and used for national competitions. The hotel's name has now been changed to 'The Inn on the Green'.

A magnificent building, Deller's Café, is remembered with affection by all Paigntonians who knew it when it functioned as the meeting place for the town's residents and holidaymakers alike. Visitors from nearby towns and villages and cadets from Britannia Royal Naval College at Dartmouth made Dellers their fashionable venue. Built by Lambshead in 1910–11 it became the town's focus for winter dinners, dances, whist drives and local organisations' parties which could number up to 1000 people at any one time. It was a sorry day for Paignton when this handsome structure was demolished in 1965. Its graceful staircases and elegant dining rooms will long be remembered.

One of the most imposing buildings on Paignton's sea front is the Redcliffe Hotel. It was originally planned by Colonel Smith who spent much of his early life in India in the Bengal Lancers. An architect and draughtsman of some repute, he came to Devon and designed the palatial buildings of Redcliffe Towers which was completed in 1864. Produced on a lavish scale and expensively furnished, it fulfilled Robert Smith's ambitions. After his death Redcliffe Towers was sold to Paris Singer (in 1877) who later sold it in 1902. From then on extensive alterations were carried out to convert the building into the superb hotel which we see today.

Following the First World War and amid the depression years of 1926–29, seaside holidays were a vital antidote to national despondency but even cut-price offers from hotels were barely affordable. The likes of the Redcliffe and Esplanade Hotels would not have been accessible to most. But then came the camping era with basic services at a price most could afford. The idea caught fire, stimulating enthusiasm all over the country. Overnight, good camps, mediocre camps and salubrious camps appeared like mushrooms. Some prospered, some simply existed but many sank without trace.

The Esplanade Hotel

ↁ THE ESPLANADE ↂ

This row of tall houses on the sea front was built around 1890 and now comprises the Esplanade with many of the residences converted into hotels. Just out of sight on the far left was the popular Hydro Hotel.

Right: *The Esplanade and beach, showing the famous mechanical elephant enjoyed for years by children visiting the area.*

Below: *An advertisement for the Hydro Hotel.*

The Hydro Hotel.

⤫ DELLER'S CAFÉ ⤫

The staircases and front entrance of Deller's Café which was demolished in 1965.

⤔ REDCLIFFE HOTEL ⤕

This picturesque Indian fantasy is the Redcliffe Hotel on Paignton's sea front.

∽ REDCLIFFE HOTEL ∾

An aerial view showing the hotel's grounds, boundaries and proximity to the sea.

∽◌ HOLIDAY CAMPS ◌∽

A happy group of holiday makers at Paignton's Kings Ash Holiday Camp in 1965

*A small part of Pontins' South Devon Holiday Camp at Paignton in
the 1950s – a little cul-de-sac of chalets with a nicely trimmed lawn.*

∾ DOWN BY THE SEA: THE VICTORIAN ERA ∾

*Paignton Harbour and a number of schooners safely secured with their sails furled.
These vessels mainly plied along the coastal waters from one county to another.*

*Paignton Harbour Cottages which date back to the early 1800s. These were mainly used as homes for the
Preventive men of Customs and Excise who operated from here to patrol the coast within their
boundaries. The Smuggler's Act of 1863 created the establishment of Preventive and Revenue men to
stop the contraband of brandy, tobacco and tea being landed without paying tax.*

❧ DOWN BY THE SEA: THE VICTORIAN ERA ❧

A distant view of Paignton Harbour taken in the early 1880s from the elevation of what is now Cliff Road. Glaringly conspicuous is the absence of buildings along the sea front and particularly on the far hills forming the skyline.

This view from the pier is of Paignton Sands and although showing only a few bathing machines at this time, they played an essential part in the by-laws on bathing at public beaches. In 1877 a law was passed that no bathing was allowed between 10a.m. and 6p.m. unless from a machine. In 1881 a man was fined for approaching within 100 yards of a lady bathing. After the First World War the wheels of the machines were removed and the machines themselves sold as garden sheds.

∽ DOWN BY THE SEA: THE VICTORIAN ERA ∾

*Guide to 'Paignton and its Attractions',
published in 1885.*

Paignton and its Attractions.

"LET us pop over to Paignton," quoth my old friend, as the Prussian band at Torquay played the National Anthem, denoting to those happy in the non-possession of watches that it was one o'clock—and dinner-time. His Solar Majesty was broad-humoured and genial, and the Strand was holding fast to its ancient and time-honoured appellation of "Frying-pan-row." There was a gentle ripple on the water, and beneath the fanning breeze pleasure-boats slanted gracefully as they plashed merrily over the wavelets with a "feather" at their bows. Now there are various means of "popping over" to Paignton—to use the expression which has a true Devonian ring about it. You may proceed by train; but this involves a good mile walk to the railway station, a long stretch of which is at the foot of a cliff; and the trudge, though charming enough in cooler moments, is hardly to be chosen in the eye of the sun. Besides, as a native passenger observed to me the other day, "Lor' a-massy, 'tan't no 'ride at all. Vath, yew be no zooner in the train than yew'm out'aun agne." Then there is the omnibus route, which affords a pleasant change, and charming variety of scenery; and "thirdly," as the parsons say, there are the steam-launches, one of which we now hear piping merrily away at the head of the new pier. By the steam-launch, accordingly, we "popped over to Paignton," the voyage seeming ever so short by reason of the pleasure it afforded. As the "Queen of watering-places" receded in the distance—like as one looking through a telescope reversed—the picture suggested a parterre of white forget-me-nots embedded in a setting of deep green moss, the villas rearing above each other in tiers, each in its own luxuriant shrubbery. In a quarter of an hour or so the two and a-half miles voyage on the lovely bay is crossed, and we heave gently alongside the promenade pier, which, with its handsome pavilion and billiard-saloon, stands out some 750 feet from one of the finest and most extensive esplanades in the kingdom.

Standing at the extreme end of this pier, where sweet melodies mingle with the soft summer air, answering to the cadences of the waves which murmur at our feet, it is natural that the recollection should be carried back, say for how long? A quarter of a century, when crinolines were in vogue, and our lady friends shrouded their pretty faces in "uglies?" Just then the "iron road" had pierced its way through the sandstone cliffs and along the ruddy ridges to Paignton, and the country folk kept high holiday on the Green as waggons laden with meat and bread and cider were drawn towards the foreshore, followed by an enormous pudding weighing a ton and a-half, and made in accordance with the traditions of the Paignton jubilee. Through the haze of memory I still see the uncouth "navvies" scrambling for their share of that famous pudding, while the rustics from the country-side—from Marldon, Stoke Gabriel, and more distant villages—fought amain for "hunks" of the pasty compound, as souvenirs of an event which was to play so important a part in the history of the place. There was no pavilion pier then, and the Green was an unkempt and shaggy piece of waste fringing the marshes and the osier beds which lay between it and the quaint little village at the foot of the verdure-clad and wooded hills.

But public and private enterprise have transformed this erst howling wilderness into a select and dignified watering-place, the fame of whose sands, and the salubrity of whose climate, are spoken of even in the remotest corners of our empire. The Green, now placed under the control of the Local Board, in trust for ever as a public recreation ground, presents a boldness and extent of marine frontage which may well excite the envy of rival seaside resorts. Around it have sprung up with almost mushroom-like rapidity handsome villas and terraces of houses, which tell of a growing popular favour in behalf of Paignton as a place of residence; whilst on the hillsides and nearer the town building operations are in full swing, testifying to the gradual development of what is to become one of the most favourite spots along the whole line of the British coast. But more of this anon; we shall pass that way presently.

What a breadth and beauty of natural loveliness stretches out beneath our gaze as we sit in the shadow of the pavilion, whence comes music stealing the whole day long. Throwing its arms wide apart on either side is the lovely bay—which travellers agree is unsurpassed for beauty even by that of Naples itself—and along the horizon formed by the English Channel big ships travel over the trackless pathway of the sea, bound for distant shores, or returning laden with the products of sunny isles and warmer climes. At the southern extremity of the bay stand the beetling cliffs of Berry Head, once, according to the chroniclers, a Roman camp, and more recently a garrison, when Devonshire folk were in a chronic state of panic lest "old Boney" should come with his legions and pay them an unpleasant visit. Nestling in an adjacent gorge are seen the town and harbour of Brixham, half hidden by a forest of tawny sails; but in an hour or so, if the wind freshens, those hardy trawlers will be far away in the offing, adding

∾ DOWN BY THE SEA: THE EDWARDIAN ERA ∾

The sea front in 1910. The long dresses and the fancy parasols are a clear indication of the date of this bygone scene. The two forms of transport on the promenade contrast sharply with one another at this time when the era of the horse-drawn cab was passing away to be replaced by the motorcar.

A happy scene at Paignton Sands in 1913. Sand, sea and deck chairs,
ice creams and donkey rides. What more could one ask for?

∽◌ DOWN BY THE SEA: THE EDWARDIAN ERA ◌∾

Donkey rides down on the sea front, early 1900s.

The sea front at the turn of the century. On the left of the picture the Green is well occupied by the visiting fair and in the centre by the sea wall two ice-cream sellers are having a good day.

ॐ DOWN BY THE SEA: THE EDWARDIAN ERA ॐ

This rare comic postcard was sent in 1910 and although the era of Victorian propriety was drawing to a close, this composition was considered positively immoral.

This picture of Paignton Esplanade and Sands is interesting for its absence of bathing tents. It seems that the Paignton UDC of 1905 had decided against bathing huts and strongly favoured beach tents. That year they had ordered 120 tents at a cost of £129 and were giving serious consideration to allowing mixed bathing.

〜 DOWN BY THE SEA: THE EDWARDIAN ERA 〜

The bearded gentleman in the deckchair has plenty of company with seven ladies, a baby and a nursemaid to say nothing of the dog, all set for a tent tea at Paignton Sands in 1910. Charges for tent hire at this time for one week varied from 4 shillings to 7 shillings according to season. The records show that Paignton had a 'Beach Inspector' whose wages amounted to £1 per week.

A promenade of prams, parasols and picture hats on the sea front at Paignton in 1906. More than a dozen bathing machines stand at the water's edge with demure maidens prepared to immerse their voluminous swim-suited bodies in the cold waters of the English Channel.

~ DOWN BY THE SEA: THE EDWARDIAN ERA ~

Left: Springtime at Paignton Harbour and the opportunity to repair the ravages of winter and prepare boats for summer days.

Below: Tent life on Paignton sands in 1910. It's a fine day, the sea is calm, the water warm and tents available for 5 shillings a week or £2.10.0. per season. Publicity was now playing a large part in Paignton's growth and a one penny 'Guide to Paignton' was produced. A report stated that 300 guides had been distributed and 65 letters from intending visitors received. The present circulation of guides now numbers around 250000.

ᴄᴏ DOWN BY THE SEA: 1912 – 1921 ᴏᴠ

An early summer's morning on Paignton Sea Front.
The donkey team await the arrival of the day's visitors.

Strollers pause to watch Fred Spencer's al-fresco show on Paigntons Esplanade in 1912.

⅋ DOWN BY THE SEA: 1912 – 1921 ⅋

One of the worst gales to affect the normal summer/autumn pleasantness of Paignton's sea front occurred on 17 September 1921 when a great storm turned the placid waters of Torbay into a turbulence of violent waves. Only the firmest structures withstood the heavy seas that pounded the promenade and such things as tents stood no chance. By the morning light of the 18th, little of the summer tentage was left as this picture shows.

In 1912 the town band preferred to play on top of the promenade shelter and hired a ladder to do so.

∾ DOWN BY THE SEA: 1912 – 1921 ∾

A close-up shot of Paignton Pier before the disastrous fire in June 1919.

This popular pier, built by Mr Hyde Dendy and designed by the well-known architect Mr G.S. Bridgman, was destroyed by fire on 18 June 1919, after 40 years of providing entertainment to the public. A concert party who were performing there lost all their properties and stage fittings – a sad day indeed for Paignton's sea front.

DOWN BY THE SEA: 1940s – 1950s

Above: *Rather than the open sea, some chose the little auto boats on the pier. If the motor stopped one could always get out and walk home!*

Left: *This little girl seems unafraid of the fearsome tiger. Dianne Quarrell (Dianne Martin) with her Mickey Mouse bucket has her photo taken by Paignton's official sea-front photographer with his life-like stuffed tiger.*

This picture of Paignton's sea front windmill was taken in the early 1950s. Brilliantly illuminated at night it had an attractive sign reading 'Welcome to Paignton' which appealed to many photographers.

CHAPTER 3

ENTERTAINMENT

THE GRAND OLD LADY OF PALACE AVENUE

The need for entertainment reaches far back into the annals of time, to an era when minstrels and court jesters sang or buffooned at the royal courts. To please or be pleased by the song, the dance or the play became an accepted part of a way of life and is even more so in our modern age. Paignton has much to be thankful for in that over the last 100 years, local men and women have proffered their versatile talents and skills in the theatre to entertain.

The Paignton Public Hall built on the higher elevation of Palace Avenue had its entertainment début on 12 September 1890, when well-known local artistes presented a variety programme which had the public clamouring for more. Among those who took part were such familiar names as Waycott, Rossiter and Eastley.

And it was on the resounding success of that first night that the Palace Avenue Theatre was born, which, with the passage of time, came to be known as 'The Grand Old Lady of Palace Avenue'. In the years that followed, and with a fast-growing population, several presentations of the operettas of Gilbert and Sullivan were performed, among them *The Pirates of Penzance*, *HMS Pinafore* and *The Gondoliers*. As far as the hall itself was concerned, it functioned as it was originally intended to do, as the venue for local shows, political and religious meetings, clubs, exhibitions, wedding receptions and society balls with 'carriages at eleven'.

Beneath the Public Hall is a huge cellar which was the drill hall of the local volunteers and in those days it was a thrilling sight to watch the men marching along the Avenue to the music of the Paignton Military Band.

By 1921, Jack Baker, an 'up and coming' entrepreneur, was producing Charles Heslop's professional summer show *Gay Follies*, among many

Pianist and music teacher Flo Deller.

other productions. In the depression years between the two world wars, the very talented Chlöe Gibson kept the theatre alive with her run of repertory.

With the advent of the Second World War, the Grand Old Lady found herself heavily absorbed with entertainments for the troops and for a time was christened 'Garison Theatre'. In the period from 1943–44, thousands of American troops were based in the surrounding area in training for the invasion of France. It is recorded that over a period of 18 months the Old Lady entertained 17 000 troops with free concerts in which 300 artistes gave their services. It was even whispered that Bing Crosby and Glen Miller's band with the famous tune 'In the Mood' made appearances.

Blessed with ingenious and creative talent, Jack produced Paignton's first pantomime in 1936 followed by further original pantomimes over the next 25 years and later, having met the London impresario Jeffrey Snelson, a successful partnership was sealed for the Paignton stage which lasted many years. Among those whose music and acting abilities in drama, pantomime or operettas that will long be remembered is Bill Coysh. His fine singing voice combined with a natural gift for acting established him among the top echelons of stage entertainment. Space forbids the inclusion of a formidable list of actors and actresses who gave so much pleasure with their memorable performances in popular plays, operettas, dramas, comedies, repertory and pantomime but there are a couple of names which should be mentioned here. Charles Patterson was a life member and stalwart of the activities of the Palace Avenue Theatre who gave over 60 years of untiring and devoted effort to the activities of the theatre's stage productions. Flo Deller was for many years the Paignton Operatic Society's pianist and is fondly remembered for her charming personality which endeared her to everyone with whom she came into contact. Her home was in New Street where she gave piano lessons to many Paignton children between the ages of seven and fourteen.

⊷ CONCERT PARTY ⊶

These are two of the scenes from Fred Spencer's al-fresco concert party which was performed on the sea front by the pier. The party entertained the public from 1910 to the outbreak of the First World War in 1914. It was a makeshift shelter and the acting had to compete with the extraneous noises of sea-front crowds. Revenue came from the pennies charged for sitting in the deck chairs but when the rain came the crowd ran for shelter.

Among her memoirs, she recalls one occasion when the Paignton Operatic Society's cast of *HMS Pinafore* were invited to stage a show on the deck of the old HMS *Britannia* lying in the River Dart off the college in the early days of the century. A launch met the players at Kingswear and while they were being ferried across the river they heartily sang the chorus of 'Over the Bright Blue Sea' much to the consternation of the producer who thought they should save their voices for the show.

Of course, it should never be forgotten that behind the glittering stage scenes and the sparkling performers there was a battalion of stage hands, miscellaneous helpers, fund-raisers and a host of others without whose help the theatre could never have survived. Despite much success, the last century has not been one of fair-weather sailing for the theatre but she has emerged triumphant and as a shining example of endurance, perseverance and fortitude. Long may she live through this new millennium. The pictures that accompany this text include scenes from memorable operettas or dramatic plays that were enacted at the Palace Theatre over many years.

This memorable picture of Second World War days shows members of the Paignton Palace Theatre Players giving a concert at the Canadian Convalescent Camp at Brixham in 1942. Among those in the group are Jack Everitt, George Langmead (Director), Joan, Denise and Doris Slee, Kath Langmead, Doris Bewley, Marjory Parkinson and Mrs Langmead.

The Palace Avenue Theatre, from an early postcard.

THE PUBLICATION OF THE FOUNDING OF

THE PAIGNTON PUBLIC HALL COMPANY LTD   1889

WITH ITS OPENING SHARES VALUE

THE PAIGNTON PUBLIC HALL COMPANY,
LIMITED.

CAPITAL £3,500, divided into 3,500 Shares of £1 each,
Of which 2/6 per Share will be payable on Application, 2/6 on Allotment, and the
balance as required, by calls not exceeding 5/- per Share.

Directors.

WASHINGTON M. G. SINGER, Esq., Steartfield, Paignton.
JAMES ALEXANDER, M.D., Bishop's Place, Paignton.
THOMAS HORATIO HODGE, Retired Captain Bengal Marine, Moorlands, Paignton.
WILLIAM WOOD ELLIS, Ironmonger, Winner Street, Paignton.
CHARLES WILLIAM VICKERS, Surgeon, 3. Terra Nova Terrace, Paignton.

WILLIAM LAMBSHEAD, Provision Dealer, Palace Avenue, Paignton, has consented to join
the Board of Directors after Allotment.

Bankers.

THE DEVON & CORNWALL BANKING COMPANY, Limited, Paignton.

Joint Solicitors.

MESSRS. EASTLEY, JARMAN & EASTLEY.
MESSRS. BARTLETT & ROBERTS.

Secretary.

W. BROMHAM, Esq., Hon. Sec., *pro tem.*

*The publication of the founding of the Paignton Public Hall Company Ltd, 1889,
with its opening share value.*

PALACE AVENUE THEATRE PLAYS

A photograph from 1938 of Iolanthe *with*, left to right, *J.M. Skinner, Paddy Rossiter, S. Higgs.*

The Pirates of Penzance, *1972.*

ᕙᕗ PALACE AVENUE THEATRE PLAYS ᕙᕗ

Pickwick, *1966.*

The Rising Generation, *1926. Included are: John Sutton, Maidee Stevens, Marion Smart, Fred Smart, Greta Huggins, Rex Axworthy, Leo Foale and Agnes Loring.*

❧ PALACE AVENUE THEATRE PLAYS ❧

Charles Patterson is seen here with his daughter Janet, costumed for The Pirates of Penzance.

≈ PALACE AVENUE THEATRE PLAYS ≈

Scenes from presentations by the Paignton Operatic, Dramatic and Choral Society including The Student Prince *in 1957 and* Iolanthe *in 1938. Among those who took part in these and other operettas were Jill Farrant, Bruce Lochtie, Howard Backer, Yvonne Wheaton, David Marshall, Cyril Eade, Bruce Seville, Vic Tomlin, Stan Bath, Pamela Martin, Bill Coysh, Ron and Mary Williams, Phyllis Elliott, Doris and Ron Roe, Donald and Patricia Wood, June Williams, Pauline Norris, Alfred Massey, Ethel Lunn, Marjorie Marriott, Jon Finch, Norman Elliott, Eddie Campion, Chad Reed, Bruce Kent and many others.*

PALACE AVENUE THEATRE PANTOMIMES

The following two pages represent a selection of scenes from pantomimes at Paignton's Palace Avenue Theatre devised by Jack Baker and produced by Jeffrey Snelson.

Cinderella, *1937.*

Dick Whittington, *1938.*

PALACE AVENUE THEATRE PANTOMIMES

Babes in the Wood, *1939*.

Babes in the Wood, *1939*.

Repertory production, The Rivals.

THE BIJOU THEATRE
& THE GERSTON HOTEL

When the railway to Paignton was opened in August 1859 it gradually transformed the agricultural/fishing village into the seaside resort it is today. Soon speculators were buying up large slices of land near the shore for development and in the next 20 years, the population of 3000 almost doubled. Fortunately for Paignton a wealthy entrepreneur, Arthur Hyde Dendy, from Birmingham, a patron of the arts and an accomplished musician, arrived on the scene and in 1870 erected the Gerston Hotel with a lavishly equipped little theatre called The Bijou. It was here on 30 December 1879 that the world première of Gilbert and Sullivan's fourth operetta *The Pirates of Penzance* was enacted. Some 50 years later, on 30 December 1929, members of the Paignton Society performed the operetta in the Bijou as a golden jubilee tributary production.

On 31 December 1879, in the House of Commons, Prime Minster Benjamin Disraeli reported that the previous day he had attended the first performance of the new Gilbert and Sullivan operetta at Paignton, whereupon someone from the back benches asked – "Where's that?" Disraeli went on to say that having visited Paignton Pier he had won a penny and a coconut, "The machine has since been repaired", he added gravely. To cries of "shame", he also informed the House that regretfully income tax would have to be raised to fourpence in the pound! Disraeli's affinity with Paignton was not exclusively confined to his liking for Gilbert and Sullivan or the Bijou Theatre but rather to the more attractive prospect of meeting his mistress who resided in Roundham Road. However, it seems that the relationship was not all sweetness and light for at this time Disraeli was in financial straits. To overcome this embarrassing situation the lady loaned him a considerable sum of money on the condition that when death took them she would be buried between him and his wife. No records exist as to whether or not this extraordinary proviso was actually honoured in the funeral arrangements.

The Royal Bijou Theatre showing the west side of the Gerston Hotel built in 1870. This is the only known photograph of the theatre taken before the development of Victoria Street and Hyde Road. The small doorway on the left of the yard entrance was the only public access to the theatre. Mr Dendy and personal guests used the main hotel staircase.

The days of horse transport outside the Gerston Hotel, Paignton, in 1912. The street ahead is Victoria Street with Waycott's Corner on the right. The drinking fountain and the tall lamp standard are particularly evocative of the Victorian era.

THE BIJOU THEATRE & THE GERSTON HOTEL

Additions and developments over the years resulted in the Gerston Hotel as shown here with its waiting horses and carriages (c.1920). This photograph was taken prior to Messrs Woolworth's extensive rebuilding programme before they opened for business in July 1932.

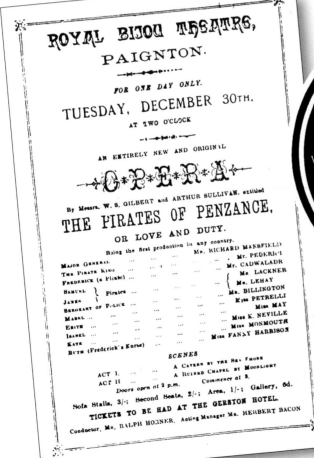

A reproduction of the original playbill and with it a copy of the commemorative plaque on the wall of the Gerston Hotel.

THE PICTURE HOUSE

Paignton's renowned and endearing old Picture House Cinema is approaching its centenary and the thoughts and memories of thousands of the town's residents must be stirred by fond reminiscences of visits to this popular centre of entertainment over the years. The Picture House was built for £4000 by the well-known builders C. and R.E. Drew who incidentally were responsible for Deller's Café and Queen's Park Mansions. On the same site and long before the cinema was erected, there stood a hotel named 'The Broadmead' which was demolished and the rubble removed all for the price of £10. When the cinema was first opened, it was called The Bioscopic Exhibition and Entertainment Centre with an added 'Suitable for Ladies'. So anxious was the cinema to preserve the proprieties of the Victorian era that unaccompanied young women were segregated by special seating arrangements – 'ladies on the left, gentlemen on the right'.

Seat prices ranged from threepence to sixpence and this included a shower of disinfectant spray at no extra charge sprayed by lady usherettes over everybody and everything including the ice creams. It was the heyday of the silent movies with epics starring Douglas Fairbanks senr, Mary Pickford, Rudolph Valentino, Pearl White and Greta Garbo. Disaster, horror and westerns were all the rage but most popular were the comedies with Charlie Chaplin, Harold Lloyd and Buster Keaton. In those days the resident pianist added the drama and love interest. At one time the Paignton Picture House had a 21-piece orchestra.

During the 1950s and '60s, the two chief projectionists at the Picture House and Regent cinemas were John Mann and Derek Waddle. Frequently, the one and only film reel of Gaumont Graphic News was due for showing at both cinemas at approxi-

mately the same time. As a result, as soon as the reel had finished at one cinema, it had to be wound back and rushed to the other in time for the scheduled programme. However, if the rail crossing gates were closed at that critical moment, delay caused chaos. Thanks to happy co-operation from the signalman, the barrier would oft-times be lifted for a few seconds to allow the news reel to cross the track to reach the other side. This was one of many hectic moments in the life of Paignton's two cinemas.

When the miracle of the first talkie arrived in 1927 it starred Al Jolson in *The Jazz Singer*. The first five words ever spoken on the screen were 'You ain't heard nothin' yet'. The second talkie was the great musical *The Broadway Melody*, thus with the advent of the vanishing 'silents' the talkies came and stayed.

Over the years, many stars of stage and television have visited and talked with John Mann, the Manager of the Picture House. Among these patrons were Agatha Christie who always had the second seat in the circle, the crime writer Edgar Wallace who would reserve a five-seater box for himself and his family, Tommy Cooper who loved ice-cream cornets but always let them thaw to liquid, Max Bygraves, Charlie Chester, Fay Dunaway, Tommy Steele, David Attenborough, Bill Owen (Compo), Danny La Rue, Bill Pertwee, Broad Forbes, Ken Dodd, Margaret Lockwood, Anne Zeigler, Webster Booth, Edward Woodward, Oliver Reed, Donald Sutherland and a host of others.

Following its closure in September 1999, the Picture House Cinema lay for a while boarded up and alone with perhaps the ghosts of those who occupied its wide screen over the decades of silent and talkie films roaming the walls. But now in the new millennium its frontage has become a ticket office for the Dart Valley Railway Co (plc), whose steam trains run from the adjacent Paignton Station to Kingswear and Dartmouth.

The Broadmead Hotel before the Picture House.

∽ THE PICTURE HOUSE ∾

The building as it was originally...

...and as it was before closure.

FESTIVAL HALL

On 2 February 1937, a joint meeting of the Chamber of Commerce and the Hotels and Boarding Houses Association was held at Evans Café to consider the possibility of an alternative building to the Public Hall, later called the Palace Avenue Theatre. There was much difference of opinion as to where a building suitable for conferences and/or stage shows could be sited and the estimated cost of £30 000 was a substantial delaying factor. This notable and popular home of entertainment replaced the former Summer Pavilion which was demolished in 1965 and when it finally appeared was designed by the architect C.F.J. Thurley in the same year.

Its conception and beginnings were plagued by controversy and problems largely due to loss of part of the Green and the covenants which preserved it. There were also unexpected problems with the actual construction for although the 'piling' depth had been estimated at 35 feet it reached no less than 52 feet. Although the contractors Staverton Contractors Ltd had quoted a price of £250 000, the final cost was £400 000 with an added charge in the 1960s of £8000 for the higher banking of 800 rear seats. Despite the setbacks and higher costs, the Festival Hall proved an unqualified success for it became a mecca of star entertainment for thousands of holiday tourists and Paignton residents. In its 32 years of highly popular entertainment the Festival Hall hosted many television and stage stars among whom were Howard Keel, Harry Secombe, Johnny Mathis, Freddy Starr, Edmundo Ross, Morecombe and Wise, The Three Degrees, Roy Orbison, Donald Peers, Danny La Rue, Bette Davis, Ken Dodd, Jimmy Cricket, Ronnie Corbett, Kathy Kirby, Tommy Cooper, Sandy Powell and Bradley Walsh.

Among others who will be remembered is Leslie Crowther with his 'Come on down' expression from his television series; Larry Grayson and his constant plea 'Shut that door'; John Hanson's wonderful tenor voice bringing national fame and the versatile and beloved artiste Sheila Bernette of *The Boyfriend* days. All of these characters helped to bring Paignton to the forefront of summer entertainment establishing the resort as a leading tourist centre in the South of England.

The late Harry Secombe was one of the most down to earth. His spontaneous humour and ad-libbing improvisation were as hilarious as any prepared script. Ken Dodd would still be on stage at 12.30a.m. with most of the staff gone home. Leslie Crowther was a party animal but did a lot for charities. These and a host of others provided a euphoria of enjoyment during the hall's lifetime and will no doubt be greatly missed by theatre enthusiasts. In 1999 the Festival Hall bowed out with its last presentation *Cinderella on Ice* performed by the Russian Ice Ballet. Following this final show the hall was demolished and in its place there now stands a super cinema The Apollo, with its nine screens and seating capacity for 1650 which opened in late 1999.

Inset: *This original Association crest was designed by Suttons, together with the Secretary Miss Lavers and the Treasurer Mrs Parkinson.*

The Festival Hall.

⋘ THE FESTIVAL HALL ⋙

The Festival Hall's opening night of 9 June 1967. Presented among its other features were George Mitchell's Black and White Minstrels *and* The Television Toppers. *It was indeed a fast and spectacular show which brought thousands of people from all parts of Devon.*

Show girls on stage.

∽∂ THE FESTIVAL HALL ∂∽

Leslie Crowther 'Come on down'.

Larry Grayson 'Shut that door'.

John Hanson, 'The Voice'.

Sheila Bernette of The Boyfriend *fame.*

სა THE PAIGNTON PUDDING ๑๑

The pudding towed by a traction engine nears its destination – Paignton Green.

CHAPTER 4

SPECIAL EVENTS

THE PAIGNTON PUDDING

Commemorative occasions are ever a feature of Paignton life and it is recorded that in 1295 the King (Edward I) granted a charter to Paignton to hold a weekly market. In token payment for this royal privilege the townsfolk were required to prepare a large 'White-pot' or 'Pudding'. By the 17th century this custom had developed and took place at 50-year intervals, the pudding being shared among the poor. In a detailed record of 1819 it seems that the pudding was made from 400lbs of flour, 170lbs of suet, 140lbs raisins and 20 dozen eggs. It was boiled for three whole days in the brewing copper of the Crown and Anchor Inn and joyfully paraded through the streets of Paignton on a wagon drawn by eight oxen to the Green. There it was distributed to the poor in a ceremony attended by 8000.

Nine centuries earlier in 1086, William the Conqueror commissioned the Domesday Book and to mark Paignton's 900th birthday in 1986, John Mann, vice President of the Torbay and Dartmouth Railway Society, proposed that a Paignton Pudding event would be apt for the occasion. As a result, representatives of the local Hotels and Caterers Association and the town's many organisations met and planned the big day.

On 1 September 1986, an enormous wooden casket containing 900 miniature puddings baked by Maurice Thoren of Taylor's Bakery, Preston, and mounted on a well wagon hauled by the Dart Valley's steam engine The Paigntonian arrived in Paignton from Kingswear. Here it was off-loaded onto a road trailer and slowly hauled by a steam-driven traction engine through the streets. Its route through Torbay Road was watched by hundreds of people. Arriving on the Green, an estimated crowd of 15000 surrounded 'the pudding' accompanied by much cheering especially when the Mayor, Jimmy Mason, began the distribution.

The event attracted 13 national and international film companies who covered the spectacle from beginning to end. Paignton is proud of its 900-year-old history and especially of its pudding.

A truly memorable event on a truly memorable day,
the Paigntonian on its journey to Paignton bearing the pudding.

❧ THE AVRO MACHINE ❧

In the Spring of 1914, the Daily Mail *airmen Salmet and Raynham gave exhibition flights around the bay in their Avro machine; this had no retractable undercarriage so the wheels sometimes brushed the tops of the bushes (where the Festival Hall stood) as they were coming in to land and the spectators on the Green had to run to get out of the way.*

Below left: This was their machine and the small boy on the left (circled) is Frank Baker standing behind his father Percy Baker, well known to old Paigntonians. Frank's elder brother Jack became Paignton's impresario, producing some remarkable pantomime epics at the Palace Avenue Theatre.

Below: Hundreds of people assembled at Paignton Green on 13 April 1914 to watch the arrival of the Daily Mail's *Avro plane flown by the pilots Salmet and Raynham.*

Flying past the Redcliffe Hotel at Preston.

❧ THE AVRO MACHINE ❧

Daily Mail *aircraft at rest on Preston Sands.*

Left: *There were no permanent hangars for the* Daily Mail *aircraft giving flying exhibitions at Paignton but the Council did provide a couple of ephemeral marquees as shelter for these wonders of the age.*

Here is Raynham in 1914 in his Avro plane flying over the pier preparing to land on Paignton Green. His touch-downs usually caused panic with people having to run for their lives.

൭ CARNIVALS ൭

Above: *Paignton Carnival, 1946, and the coronation of the Harvest Queen, Joan Medway.*

Left: *Carnival Quartet, 1946, and a fitting tribute to the four services of the Second World War representing the Navy, Army, Air Force and the Land Army.*

Above: *The Harvest Queen and her three attendants Misses E.L. Wood, Joan McVicar and P.E. Rundle are paraded through the streets of Paignton.*

⊷ MISCELLANEOUS EVENTS ⊶

Over 100 people are present in this photograph of a party held at St Michael's Girls Club in Paignton on 29 November 1934 to celebrate the marriage of Princess Marina of Greece to the Duke of Kent.

Left: *This copy of a photograph taken by a holiday visitor suggests some sort of military occasion taking place with an ecclesiastical blessing at Queen's Park. The photo is dated 28 February 1907.*

Right: *Paignton really made a powerful display in the 1950s with this impressive pageantry of illumination. Even the rockery and fountain were lit up to give an exhilarating effect against the black night sky.*

ᴖ ROYAL OCCASIONS ᴖ

Left: *A celebratory arch erected in Conway Road to mark the Coronation of King George V and Queen Mary in 1911. Patriotism was very strong in those days and every opportunity was taken to commemorate a royal occasion.*

Below: *For the same occasion large crowds assembled on Paignton Green to hear patriotic speeches by local dignitaries. Commonwealth flags were flown whenever possible – how could the joyous crowds have known that within three years the lifeblood of the nation would be draining away on the fields of France in the Great War?*

Below: *The arch remained as a tourist attraction until the King's death in 1936.*

Above: *The Jubilee Arch of 1935 was sited at the entrance to the sea front to celebrate the Silver Jubilee of King George V and Queen Mary in 1935. The arch was a splendid sight especially at night when it was lit by hundreds of bulbs installed by the Paignton Electric Light Co.*

CHAPTER 5

VICTORY IN EUROPE

After over five years of the terrible trauma of the Second World War, the unconditional surrender of Nazi Germany brought peace to a war-weary Britain. It was a time of rejoicing, a time to celebrate. Street parties were held in almost every town and village in Britain. People pooled what few rations they had to revel in the euphoria of the end of hostilities and for a few weeks were bound together by a common sense of thankfulness. In Paignton, street parties were abundant.

Prior to the Allied invasion of Normandy on 6 June 1944, hundreds of thousands of American troops were based in South Devon including a large number in and around Paignton. Many bonds were forged between the GIs and local families and many marriages took place with local girls. Half a century later in June 1994, Paignton organised a period of commemoration and welcome to veteran US soldiers who survived the D-Day landings in France and came back to revisit faded memories and once familiar territories.

Paignton made every effort to stage a gregarious reception for our American Second World War cousins by doing whatever possible to present familiar sights and sounds of 1944. There were parades of American jeeps and tanks provided by the Historical Military Vehicle Association and Paignton's sea front echoed to the rumble and squeals of tank caterpillar tracks accompanied by military swing bands repetitively playing the famous Glen Miller's favourite tune 'In the Mood'.

Among those from the States who attended were veterans who had won the American Purple Heart and the Congressional Medal. It was indeed a heart-warming and memorable occasion reminding Britain of the sacrifice our Allies of many nations made to save the country and indeed the world from the despotic rule and tyranny of Nazism. As will be recognised from the following photographs, some of the events were based at the Torbay Cinema in Torbay Road, Paignton, and were organised by the Torbay and Dartmouth Railway Society.

A party of 50 in full swing in Eden Vale Road celebrating VE Day, 8 May 1945 (Victory in Europe). Among those present are Councillor Stabb, Dorothy King, Olga King, Brenda Harding, Brian Harding, Pamela Ponting and sister, Derek Ponting, Adrienne King, Tony King, June King, Edward King, Vera Grant, Ernie Grant, Tony Johnson, Colin Johnson, Violet Collins and Michael Wills.

᧧ VICTORY TEA PARTIES ᧧

Merritt Street like many others played their part too with a children's victory tea party.

Another celebration victory tea party in 1945, this time in Millbrook Street showing Littlegate Street in the background.

This Army group of the First World War is the 222 Battery of the Royal Artillery temporarily based at Paignton.
Most of these are Cornishmen from a little-known place called Nancegolan between Camborne and Helston.

The Paignton War Memorial in Palace Avenue Gardens
is unveiled by Colonel C.R. Burn ADC, MP, on 29 June 1921.

ↁ WELCOME BACK THE YANKS ↁ

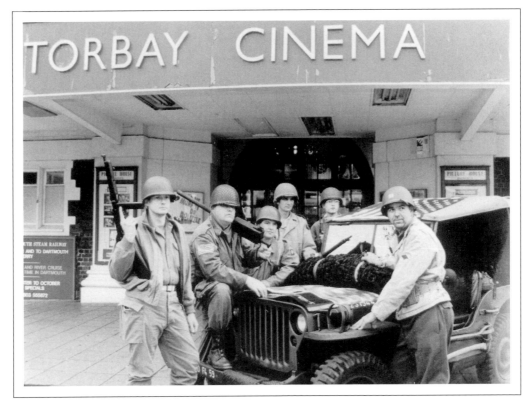

The armed reconnaissance unit ready for the 'off'. (Herald Express, *which publishes a Bygones special every Tuesday*)

'Hold it right there Punk'.

❧ WELCOME BACK THE YANKS ❧

A visiting American soldier from Montana is welcomed by uniformed troops at the Torbay Cinema.

Admiring Paigntonians queue up to meet the US Colonel.

⋘ THE WAR AT SEA ⋙

Following the surrender of the German High Seas Fleet at Scapa in 1918 when the crews sank most of their own ships in the Flow, the British towed what was left to breaker's yards. In 1920 while the tug **Warrior** *was towing two German destroyers from Cherbourg to a breaker's yard at Teignmouth, a vicious gale parted the tow. Both destroyers were driven ashore in Torbay; one on to Preston Beach and the other on to the rocks at Roundham Head. In this picture the rocks at Roundham Head firmly hold the second German destroyer. The crew of three were eventually rescued thanks to a brave coastguard employee George Pearce who struggled through the surf with ropes. For this courageous act he was awarded the magnificent sum of £1.*

The German destroyer at Preston Sands.

⊷ THE ARP ⊶

During the Second World War, such was the shortage of manpower that women were often called upon to serve in the emergency services. This unusual picture is of a women's ARP unit in Paignton in 1940.

URBAN DISTRICT OF PAIGNTON   Sector.........................

FIRE BOMB PRECAUTIONS   Group.........................

IMPORTANT OFFICIAL FORM WHICH WILL
BE COLLECTED BY AN AIR RAID WARDEN
                                            Name
                                    House.............
                                            Number
Street...

Have you a stirrup pump?...

Have you a ladder on the premises?.............................. Approximate length...............................

I, the undersigned, undertake to carry out the duties of :—
        (a) A fire watcher at the above address   AND
        (b) A member of a Supplementary Fire-fighting Party at the above address
             and in the vicinity

        Mr.
Signed Mrs...   Date.......................................
        Miss
(NOTE.—Instruction will be given to all volunteers who will be notified of the time and place at which
        to attend)   SAMUEL HODSON,
                                                                        Clerk of the Council

A copy of the official registration form for becoming an ARP warden issued by Sam Hodson, Clerk to the Council.

∽ THE ARP ∾

Air Raid Precautions groups were well supported by volunteers in the Paignton area. This contingent of 22 was responsible for the Lammas Lane district. On the right of the front row of three is Mr Frank Martin, later Mayor of Torbay.

The Preston section was even larger with the inclusion of seven ladies.

CHAPTER 6

EDUCATION

HAYES ROAD PRIMARY SCHOOL

Hayes Road Primary School opened on 18 November 1935. The following pictures of pupils and teachers cover the period from 1952 to 1983 and have been kindly loaned by the head-mistress at the time of writing, Mrs Morgan.

Right: *Infants Christmas Party, c.1953.*

Selected pupils pay a visit to Oldway Mansion in the 1960s. Left to right, back: Mr Slater (headmaster), Cllr Walke (Mayor), Cllr Snell, Mrs Richard (teacher), Mr Walmsley (Chief Education Officer).

cro HAYES ROAD PRIMARY SCHOOL cro

The pupils of 1968 with teacher Mr Hoyle.

The pupils of 1970 with teacher Mrs Richards.

School Sports Day, 1973.

◈ HAYES ROAD PRIMARY SCHOOL ◈

The pupils of 1973 with teacher Mrs Preece.

The pupils of 1975 with teacher Miss Swift.

The pupils of 1976 with teacher Mr Thompson.

❧ HAYES ROAD PRIMARY SCHOOL ❧

The pupils of 1977 with teacher Mr Peacock.

The musical group, 1979, with teacher Mr Greg Thompson.

Teacher's at the school, 1983. Left to right, back: Greg Thompson, unnamed student teacher, Gwen Fletcher, Olga Ellison, Tony Peacock, Clare Marshall, Marjorie Benjamin, Jan Swift, John Celly (headmaster); front: Joan Pennell, Barbara Preece, Margaret Northcott, Geraldine Hooper, Helen Peters, Cherralyn Taylor, Jill Greenwell, Candy Smith.

❧ COLLATON ST MARY PRIMARY SCHOOL ❧

These old pictures of young pupils of the primary school of Collation St Mary span a period of some 40 years, most of whom lived in Paignton. The names are unknown but perhaps some may recognise themselves or be recognised by friends or relatives.

Left and below:
*Collaton St Mary
Primary School, 1920s.*

The school in the 1940s.

ɷ COLLATON ST MARY PRIMARY SCHOOL ɷ

The pupils during the 1950s.

Nativity Play, Collaton Primary School, 1960s.

ɷ OSNEY GIRLS' SCHOOL ɷ

This is a very old photograph of the pupils of Osney Girls' School
(off the Torquay Road) dating back to the late 1890s.

ఴ MARIST CONVENT SCHOOL ఴ

Marist Convent School was built by Henry John Bailey in 1890 who also built the Pot Black Club in Winner Street, the Tropicana in Winner Street and the Coniston in Sands Road. The Marist sisters bought the house in 1908 and, after enlargement in 1930, it closed in 1932. Later it opened as Tower House School.

This photograph shows Marist Convent School around 1920.

A peep into a classroom at Marist as it was in the 1920s. Note the teacher's rostrum, the old blackboard and easel, and the old-fashioned desks.

PAIGNTON ZOO

Devika the cub.

Above: *Suma the tiger.*

Right: *Pertinax contemplates the human race.*

Below: *Duchesse and Gay.*
Friendly frolics in the farmyard.

CHAPTER 7

FREE TIME

PAIGNTON ZOO

Paignton can be justifiably proud of its Zoological and Botanical Gardens, home to some of the world's most endangered animals. Covering nearly 100 acres, the zoo is undoubtedly the area's biggest attraction welcoming over 400 000 visitors a year. The fact that over 1000 animals occupy its extensive grounds places the zoo among the top four in the country. Because of its long-sighted approach to the conservation of our global wildlife heritage it is now registered as an Environmental Park with the objective of safeguarding what is left of the world's animal population; a kingdom that is being steadily destroyed at an alarming rate by the greed and indifference of mankind. This protective aim is being achieved by means of a comprehensive programme of education, captive breeding, research and conservation of natural habitats.

To this end, Paignton Zoo welcomes around 35 000 schoolchildren and others on educational trips each year and by this method gives each and every visitor an abiding message about the world's wildlife and the urgent need for protection of its eroding environment. But this is just one part of its purpose for it seeks to counteract the losses already sustained over many years. Through research as part of a global network of zoos and botanical gardens it now contributes towards national and international programmes for conservation. Recently, the zoo reached the end of a £6 million Euro-funded improvement programme transforming it into a park of the living world with many improved and natural habitats.

In 1955, upon the death of the founder of the Zoo, Herbert Whitley, a charitable scientific and educational trust was formed. Known as the Herbert Whitley Trust it now owns the Zoo Gardens, and has developed a world-wide reputation as a non-profit-making institution with a mission for education and conservation. Such is the zoo's international renown for its unique collection of wildlife, that it has imperceptibly assumed an ambassadorial role in playing host to large numbers of people of every race, colour and creed. It is undoubtedly true that Herbert Whitley's vision has played a significant part in placing Paignton on the national and international map.

An aerial view of the zoo and botanical gardens.

97

∾ MUSICAL GROUPS ∾

The Curledge Street Girl's Choir of 1949.

Founder members of Kingsley Male Voice Choir at the Paignton Park Hotel on 1 November 1949 for their first dinner. The photograph includes, from left to right standing: *Pat Fowman, Owen Stephens, ? Paling, E. Lane, Walter Bourne, Harold Hedges, Edward Collins, Percy Frain, Bert Hutchins, Wilfred Trute, ? Underhay, Bill Hawkin, Stan Bath, Cliff Pritchard, Gerald Allen, Charlie Tucker, Harold Read, Leslie Quarrell, Percy Pearse;* seated: *Eileen Burn, Dr Barnes, Winnie Saunders.*

මය MUSICAL GROUPS ඉන

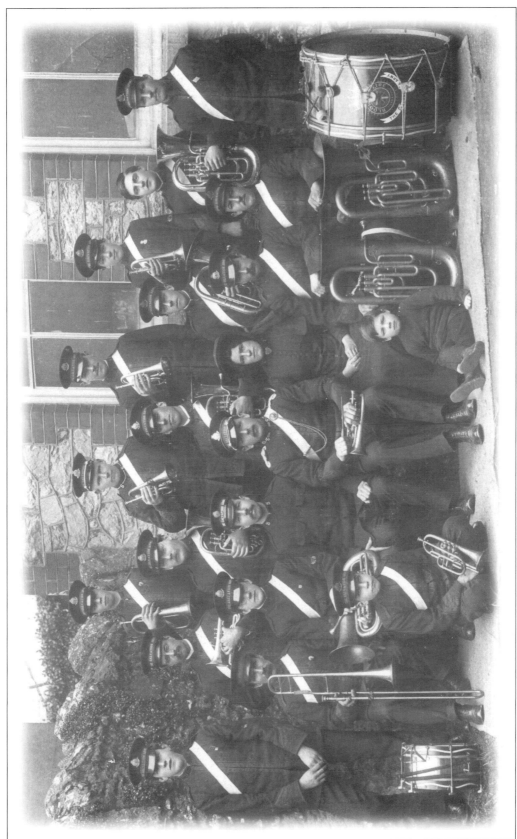

Paignton Salvation Army was well supported in the early 1900s, and here are the band members with a variety of expensive instruments in March 1913.

⋄ MUSICAL GROUPS ⋄

*The entire Methodist Church Choir assemble for an 'al fresco' group photograph in the early 1970s.
Front row centre is the Reverend Arnold Belwood.*

*The view of Paignton sea front as seen from the elevated Roundham area showing the pier
and bandstand. The distant hills of Barcombe are noticeably bare of houses, c.1888.*

∽ YOUNG MEN'S GROUPS ∾

When this photograph was taken the YMCA was a very strongly supported association.
Here at Oldway are some of its members during a rally in July 1921.

Paignton's First Company of the Boys' Brigade, 1925–26. Left to right, back: F. Martin, B. Parnell,
E. Davies, S. Kenyon, S. Allen, A. Macmurdo, S. Penwill, J. Harris, C. Eager, W. Kitchen, W. Dodd, G. Ford;
middle: I. Allen, G. Stidworthy, C. Hooper, L. Quarrell, Captain A. Matthews, E. Passmore, O. Stevens,
F. Webber, G. Ford; front: M. Crimp, H. Cudmore, J. Land, T. Salter, W. Taylor, W. Williams.

୫ PAIGNTON SWIMMING CLUB ୭

Among those who have guided and organised the Paignton Swimming Club throughout the last 40 or 50 years, acting either as President, Chairman or Secretary, are such names as Harry Truscott, Jack Scott-Ormsby, Gladys Elliott, Betty Tucker and Harold Allan. It was from the unstinting efforts of these and many others who lifted and maintained the reputable sportsmanship of swimming in Paignton and spent hours at the bathside teaching children and young people to swim, that the standard of club and county championships was raised to the high levels of today. The following pictures will stir memories of past events.

The occasion of the 1967 prize-giving of Trophy Awards at St George's Hall, Three Beaches, Goodrington. Among those in the rear rows are Alfie Steart (President), Betty Tuckett, Brian Hill, Roy Hoare, Harold Allan (Chairman), Gladys Elliott and Stella Margetts of Torquay Leander.

Paignton Swimming Club's Juniors at Pontins Holiday Camp Swimming Pool. Among those present are Brian Hill, Betty Tuckett, Harry Truscott, Mark Pearce, Roy Hoare and Dianne and Sarah Stevens.

⊱ PAIGNTON SWIMMING CLUB ⊰

Left: *Trophy Awards for 1970. Among those pictured are: John Truscott, Susan Truscott, Gary Conway, Janice Green, Vivienne Waterhouse, Margaret Williams, Deborah Thursk, the Cressells and the Hoare children.*

Below: *The Easter Swimming Course at Pontins Camp, 1966. In the front row are the organisers Gladys Elliott and Jack Scott-Ormsby.*

Below: *Members of Paignton Swimming Club of 90 years ago. Two world wars and several generations later the club has not only maintained but advanced the standard of county swimming.*

❧ PAIGNTON ROWING CLUB ❧

Below: *Paignton Regatta, 1957. A number of the crew and committee in preparation for the race. Left to right, back (crew members):* Bob Salter, Jimmy Modgridge, Harry Downs, Denis Budd; *front (fixing rigger):* Ken Ford and Mr Hill.

Above: *Paignton Rowing Club, the novice's crew, 1956. Left to right, back:* Gordon Trust, John Way, David Teague, Rod Cose; *in front:* Francis ? (cox).

Paignton Rowing Club, Junior Crew, Totnes, 1957. Left to right:
Francis ? (cox), Mike Reynolds, Rod Cose, Roy Fletcher, Dave Teague.

Paignton's ongoing support and encouragement for its Rowing Club is clearly reflected in this memorable old photo of one of the their party/dance occasions in the 1930s.

∽ PAIGNTON BOWLING CLUB ∾

Paignton Bowling Club, Open Day, 1969. Those present include: W.H. Hitchman, F. Snow, W. Barnes, G. Cornelius, P. Ellison, G. Langlands, A.S.L. Force, G. Rice, C. Dale, C. Jennings, D. Boutcher, F. Drake, C. Whitehouse, D. Goldsborough, T. Scollay, A. Barker, F. Battershill, E. May, H. Frame, F. Foster, Mrs Pering, Mrs Johnston, C. Summerhayes, Mrs Battershill, Mrs Jemmett, T. Kingan, R. Watts, A. Harris, Mrs Bennett, Mrs Jennings, Mrs Curtis, Mrs Smith, Mrs D. Williams, Mrs Wilsdon, A. Codling, F. Chapple, Mrs Southam, Mrs English, Mrs Tupper, Mrs Poulson, Mrs Rice, Mrs Crouch, Mrs Reynolds, Mrs Gibson, Miss Williams, Mrs Frame, Mrs Scollay, B. Lang, L. Wilsdeon, A. Williams, H. Goodall, W. Tidy, W. Plaice, H. Oke, C. Williams, C. Bowled, D. Russ, H. English, P. Pering, E. Rudd, R.T.E. Perkins, J.W. Clayton, C.E. Ashworth, R.H. Johnston.

Members spanning 70 years of the club's history meet in 1992 to celebrate its 90th anniversary.

∽ PAIGNTON BOWLING CLUB ◡

The Paignton Bowling Club 60 years earlier around the 1930s.

Although Paignton Green has been used for many and varied events this photograph shows the Green being prepared for a bowling tournament around 1925.

∓ PAIGNTON ATHLETICS ∘

A sightseeing crowd on Paignton Green in the 1930s watching the Regatta Sports events.

Annual Regatta sports day on Paignton Green with an audience of supporters.
The race appears to be a 200-yard open for men with five actually competing.

෴ PAIGNTON ATHLETICS ෴

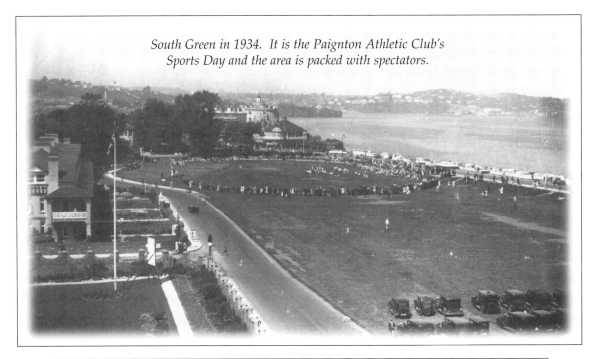

*South Green in 1934. It is the Paignton Athletic Club's
Sports Day and the area is packed with spectators.*

*Members of the Paignton Athletic Club at Queen's Park proudly showing off this handsome
solid-silver cup which they won in the Exeter to Exmouth Road Relay Race in 1966. In the mid
1960s the Paignton Club were riding on the crest of a wave, winning one event after another. The
cup as shown was known as the Exmouth Chamber of Trade Commerce Trophy.* Left to right,
back: *Tom Hennessey, Arthur Toms, Reg Hudson, Bill Cann (senr), Bob McMasters, ?, Ivan
Martin, ?, Ray Roper, Bill Valentine, Bill Cann (junr), Bill Pearse;* front: *Denis Crook, Trevor
Honeychurch, Peter Perry, Mark Watts, Alfie Cox.*

൭ PAIGNTON ATHLETICS ൭

The Paignton Amateur Athletic Club, c.1930. In the centre is Syd Cooksley and on his left Harold Pearson and Arthur Toms. Among the rest are Raymond Hole, Jack French, Charlie and Millie Gilbert, Jack Waters and Bill Bridgman.

An athletics meeting at Queen's Park in the early 1900s. The event appears to be a 200-yards handicap race over ten hurdles. There are four competitors; the leading three are at hurdle number three while 'scratch' man is clearing hurdle one. On estimate there must be almost 1000 spectators present including those in the stands and pavilion. The judges' tables are centre ground with a catering tent to the far left.

ᏜᎦ PAIGNTON ATHLETICS ᏜᎦ

Another sports day at Queen's Park at the turn of the century. There appears to be a long-distance race going on with three competitors on the far right following the boundaries of the course.

Paignton Amateur Athletic Club team and officials in 1966 at their annual prize-giving reception at Oldway with the Chairman of the Paignton Urban District Council, Councillor Kenneth Walke. Left to right: Sheila Thomson, Ivan Martin, Cllr Kenneth Walke, Dennis Crook, Bill Ann senr, Trevor Honeychurch, Arthur Toms, Peter Perry, Bill Pearse, Mr Watts, Reg Hudson, Bill Cann junr.

⁊ FOOTBALL ⁊

Paignton Town's AFC Team, 1952. Left to right, back: Reg Creber, John Cunningham, Brian Carter, Jumbo Ali Khan, Ron Fenton, Len Thomas; front: John Roper, Peter Crewe, Frank Smith, Brian Harris, Joe Halligan.

A snapshot of Ron Fenton in action on Paignton Green in earlier days

⊸ FOOTBALL ⟩∞

Paignton Harriers outside Queen's Park Pavilion in 1966. Left to right: Mark Watts, Bill Valentine, Dennis Crook, Peter Whitworth, Trevor Honeychurch, Reg Hudson, ?, Gerry Chase, Tim Hennessey, Ivan Martin.

Footballs still had laces when this photo was taken back in the 1950s. Paignton's team at that time included the following players, left to right back: *Fred Tucker, Ron Fenton, Ken Peters, Frank Smith, Mike Cavanna, Don Piper;* front: *Eddie Piper, Den Moysey, Brian Harris, Bernard Clarke, Brian Tyler.*

৩ RUGBY ৩

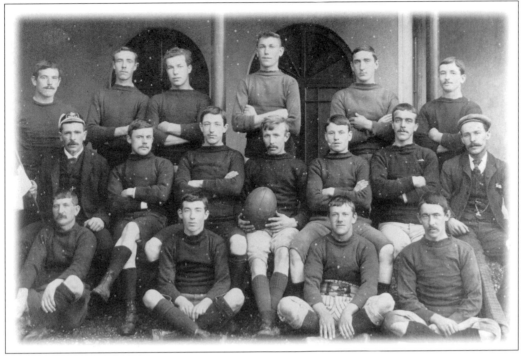

*Paignton's Rugby Club history can be traced back to the early 1900s.
Here is a championship '15' with a few of their older colleagues in 1905.*

*Paignton's first rugby team to be formed after the First World War. The picture
was taken in 1919 and most of these players must have served in the conflict.*

∽◯ CRICKET ◯∾

Right: *Not the bridge over the River Kwai but the bridge over the watercourse in Victoria Park. Paignton's Cricket Club team of 1902 take a well-earned rest on the old rustic bridge. The club will soon be celebrating its centenary.*

Left: *Paignton Cricket Club's team as it was at the outbreak of the Second World War, 1939.*

Right: *The ladies of the Paignton Cricket Club enjoy a quiet cup of tea while the men enjoy a second innings. Left to right: Chris Ashworth, Vera Benton, Chris Robinson, ?, Jackie Smith, Joyce Post, Pat Fuller, Pam Fenton, Margaret Baker, Vera Wilson, Mary Whitburn.*

∽ PAIGNTON SAILING CLUB ∾

Above: *Paignton Sailing Club yachts in Paignton Harbour unfurling their sails in readiness for a day's racing in the 1930s.*

Left: *Paignton Sailing Club Regatta Committee about 1945, in the grounds of Cliff House. Included are: Caleb Lewis, Dr Butler, Edward Trewin, Capt Matthey, H. Drew, Major S. Vickers, W.E. Forster and Captain Bennett.*

Left: *Paignton Sailing Club Regatta Committee about 1952, on Roundham Head (Cliff House in background). Included are: Pat Tapp, Walter Bessant, Major A. Waycott, Jack Edmonds, Christopher Holmes, Captain Money and Alan Cummings.*

PAIGNTON SAILING CLUB

Left: *An exciting finish for the Paignton Sailing Club's yachts in the Paignton Regatta in Torbay, August 1923.*

Below: *Paignton Sailing Club, Centenary Year Commemorative Programme.*

Left: *Programme for Paignton Regatta, 1933.*

An undated photograph of a regatta at Paignton.

CHAPTER 8

OLDWAY MANSION & PRESTON

OLDWAY MANSION

Paignton undoubtedly owes much to its benefactor Isaac Merritt Singer (1811–73), the sewing machine millionaire who built the magnificent Oldway Mansion at nearby Preston. The fact that it is one of the most photographed buildings of its kind in the county makes it a leading and regular tourist attraction to thousands of visitors every year. Singer originally nicknamed this remarkable building 'The Wigwam' which, together with its gardens, comprised 19 acres of land.

While he may not have been the actual inventor of the sewing machine it was without doubt Isaac's innovative mind that made it a world-wide success. He became the first man to mass produce and mass market one of the greatest boons of the industrial age. Financially successful, by 1860 at the age of 49 he had amassed a personal fortune of 13 million dollars.

Isaac Merritt Singer was not only a legend in his own lifetime but a giant of America's Industrial Revolution. His personal life was not without interest; he fathered 24 children and maintained three mistresses, as well as marrying twice legally. Having had to flee from America because of his philandering activities and bigamy, he arrived in France and there met, married and had six children with Isabelle Boyer who was later chosen to be the model for the statue of Liberty. The children were Mortimer, Winnaretta, Washington, Paris, Isabelle Blanche and Franklin. Following the invasion of France by the Prussians in 1870, he brought his family to England, and to Paignton, where he purchased several acres of land, including an inn, some cottages, and a villa in which he lived, now known as Little Oldway.

The foundation stone of Oldway Mansion was laid by Isaac's wife Isabella in May 1873 and although the building of it was in the hands of the local architect George Bridgman, Isaac Singer adopted a firm control over the construction. A clause in the contract stated that should a strike occur, the building work would stop immediately. This was in the days when there was only parish relief for the unemployed. It was said that he also supplied different coloured uniforms for the workforce so that he would know who was doing what job. There was little possibility of a strike, however, as Singer paid higher wages than the Council who were highly embarrassed by labour shortages.

One of Isaac Singer's passions was horses and in the area opposite the entrance to the Mansion he erected a large round building solely for their stabling called The Rotunda. No expense was spared for its ready, easy and frequent conversion for alternative uses, with a balcony for spectators, swimming pool and a removable wooden floor. This enabled Isaac to give parties on a lavish scale for Paignton children, even on one or two occasions hiring a complete circus for their entertainment.

Isaac is buried in the family mausoleum in the Torquay cemetery having left four sons, Mortimer (knighted in 1920 to become High Sheriff of Berkshire), Washington (High Sheriff of Wiltshire), Paris and Franklin. Such was the esteem and respect bestowed on Isaac that at his funeral the line of carriages stretched for nearly two miles. His fortune at the time was said to be in excess of £15 million.

Inset: *Isaac Merritt Singer in his later years.*

∾ OLDWAY MANSION ∾

Two views of Oldway Mansion.

ᦒ OLDWAY MANSION ᦒ

Right: *Issac Merritt Singer, who lived at Little Oldway.*

Little Oldway.

The Rotunda in 1873, a pavilion for horses.
Inside was a swimming pool tiled with a surround of Sicilian marble.

❧ OLDWAY MANSION ❧

Above: *Laying of the foundation stone for Oldway Mansion by Isabella Singer in 1873.*

Left: *Singer's prototype sewing machine, 1850.*

Right: *Isabella Singer and four of their six children, c.1870.*

The Singer family in fancy dress in Oldway's ballroom, c.1900. Paris is absent from the group but his wife Lily is seen reclining at the front with Winnaretta (later Lady Leeds) top left.

Isaac and Isabella Singer with Winnaretta and Franklin, c.1872.

PARIS SINGER:
A NEW GENERATION

Sadly, Isaac Singer was not destined to live in his new home, dying shortly before its completion in 1875. Oldway Mansion as it is today is the work of Isaac's third son Paris, who in the tradition of his father spent another fortune in remodelling it in the style of the finest building he knew, the Palace of Versailles, and with hints of buildings in the French capital's Place de Concorde.

Paris Singer, aged 35.

Paris Singer is probably the best known of Isaac's sons because of his close involvement in the welfare of Paignton, not only as a developer but with much of the building in the area and as a generous benefactor to many worthy causes including St John's Church, Paignton Hospital and the poor of the town. At the early age of 19, Paris had married a striking beauty in Australia named Lily Graham. After their marriage in 1887 he brought his bride back to England where they raised a family of four boys and a girl – Herbert, Cecil, Pat, George and Winnaretta, who became Lady Leeds.

The interior of Oldway is dominated by a great, branching multi-coloured marble staircase. Above it is one of the main attractions, a magnificent painted ceiling, supported by columns with gilded capitals, spiral shapes or volutes and with a splendid ornamental moulding that runs around it.

By 1909, Paris, aged 42, had separated from his wife and met the celebrated dancer Isadora Duncan. They quickly became lovers and embarked upon a passionate but turbulent affair which lasted for eight years. However, despite all his entreaties Isadora refused to marry Paris and in that age of probity and moral integrity the relationship became an international scandal. Although she remained his mistress for many years, when they embarked upon a trial marriage it ended in failure. Tragedy was to follow in 1913 when their son Patrick, aged two, and his half-sister were drowned when the car in which they were travelling plunged out of control into the River Seine. Ironically, Isadora herself was to die in a car accident in Nice in 1927 at the age of 49. As a passenger in a Bugatti car, the long scarf she was wearing became entangled in one of the wheels and strangled her. In the 1960s, Oldway was used for the shooting of the film *Isadora* in which, among other actresses, Vanessa Redgrave starred.

Paris Singer and his wife Lily after their marriage in 1887.

Lily Singer, from a portrait by Pal Mathey, c.1895.

❧ PARIS SINGER: A NEW GENERATION ❧

Left: *The staircase.*

Above: *A corner of the ceiling at Oldway.*

Below: *The jewel in the crown of the interior is the gigantic painting (30ft x 18ft) of the crowning of Josephine which is a copy of the original by Jaques Louis David and forms a spectacular backdrop to the staircase. Bought by Singer in 1898, it was sold back to the Palace of Versailles in 1946 and a reproduction bought and restored to its original position at Oldway in 1995.*

ISADORA

Isadora and son Patrick.

Left: *Isadora days before her death in France.*

Isadora Duncan (1878–1927).

'Adieu mes mais je vais a la Gloire.'

Left: *The death of Isadora Duncan at Nice, September 1927, being acted by Vivian Pickles in 1966. The driver said 'I have killed the Madonna'.*

WAR & BEYOND

At the outbreak of the First World War, Paris Singer personally paid for the conversion of Oldway into a military hospital with over 100 rooms placed at the disposal of doctors and nurses to be allocated for the use of the wounded from the battlefields of Flanders. Winnaretta played her part by employing her time as one of the nurses.

Following the Battle of the Somme in 1915, the number of beds was increased to 255, and Paignton received its first visit by a member of the Royal family when Queen Mary (wife of King George V) arrived on a tour of inspection to see for herself the conditions and treatment of the wounded.

In the years following the end of hostilities, Paris Singer and his family no longer lived at the Mansion and in 1927 it became the headquarters of the Torbay Country Club. Over the next 12 years the clouds of another club were gathering with the rise of Nazism led by Adolf Hitler. By 1939 the world was plunged into the abyss of the Second World War which by 1945 had resulted in the killing of 60 million people. It was during this period that Oldway, once again, became involved in wartime life when the mansion was transformed into a centre for one of the many training wings of the Royal Air Force and the Commonwealth.

The end of the Second World War and the termination of Oldway as a temporary wartime unit marked the end of Paris Singer's time in England and

Lord and Lady Leeds.

the start of an inspired new venture in the United States of America where he adopted citizenship, building a new hospital as a patriotic gesture towards his new home, where his father before him had created his fame and fortune.

But what was to become of Paignton's beloved Oldway Mansion? At that time, Paignton's Council Offices were dispersed to various places around the town making control of administration difficult. To gather these departments into one cohesive centre, the Council purchased the whole of the Oldway Estate which included the Mansion, Little Oldway, the Rotunda, the bowls pavilion and 19 acres of grounds including two bowling greens, six hard tennis courts, thirteen grass courts, a croquet lawn, several gardens and the terraces – the purchase price for the whole magnificent package being £46 000. On 18 December 1946, the official opening ceremony was performed by Lady Leeds (Winnaretta Singer, granddaughter of Isaac Merritt Singer); a great occasion indeed with the Council worthy inheritors of this splendid establishment.

A large number of rooms at Oldway have now been converted into Torbay Council offices, while on the ground floor the Civic Society is creating a Heritage Room with information on the history of Paignton and the Singer family. The people of Paignton are justifiably proud of this elegant architectural edifice which stands as a monument to a history of achievement, drama, hope and despair, tragedy and joy.

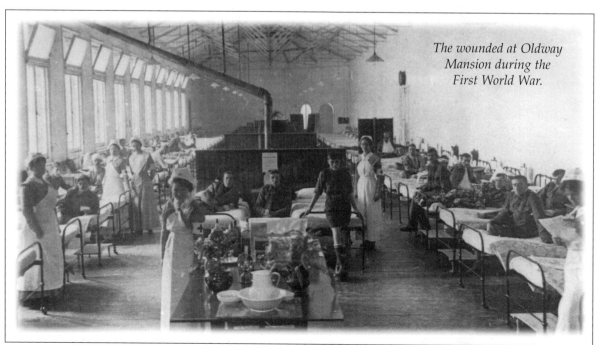

The wounded at Oldway Mansion during the First World War.

∽ OLDWAY'S WOUNDED ∾

*The wounded at
Oldway Mansion
during the
First World War.*

৬ OLDWAY'S WOUNDED ৬

Left: *This photo is of Paignton Cottage Hospital taken around 1880 when it was being supported by many Paignon carnivals*

Right: *The operating surgery at the mansion's hospital.*

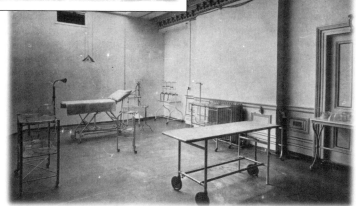

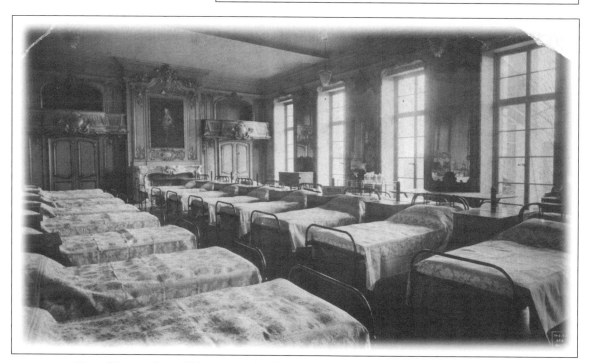

One of the wards at Oldway mansion hospital in the First World War, 1914 – 1918.

∼ COUNCIL MATTERS ∽

This is the last official photograph of the members of Paignton Urban District Council taken on 30 September 1967 at Oldway Mansion before amalgamation when the new Torbay Council was formed. Left to right, back: Fred Bidgood, Ray Snell, Frank Charlesworth, Arthur Agar, John Bewley, Graham Lorraine; middle: John Hayman, Bill Preston, Syd Elliott, Quentin Buckland, John Ellswood, Bill Chidgey, Leon Jones, Jack Bennett; front: G.K. Foster, Mrs Fraser-James, Jimmy Tremeer, Frank Martin, Ken Walker, Jack Kingsland, Wally Beasley, Mrs Heath, Mrs Walton, Mrs Basildon, John Cole;

Staff of the Paignton Urban District Council set off from outside the Council Offices for their annual outing.

⊶ COUNCIL MATTERS ⊷

OUR LOCAL AUTHORITIES FOR 70 YEARS
PAIGNTON URBAN DISTRICT COUNCIL
CHAIRMEN FROM 1906/7 TO 1967/68

1906-07	E. Westlake	1937-38	G. W. H. Spanton
1907-08	W. J. Ham	1938-39	G. W. H. Spanton
1908-09	W. J. Ham	1939-40	E. J. Powell
1909-10	H. A. Parnell	1940-41	W. J. E. Down
1910-11	F. Sarson	1941-42	W. J. E. Down
1911-12	W. J. Ham	1942-43	W. J. E. Down
1912-13	W. J. Ham	1943-44	G. Stabb
1913-14	W. J. Ham	1944-45	G. Stabb
1914-15	R. Moore	1945-46	G. Stabb
1915-16	J. H. Cooper	1946-47	G. Stabb
1916-17	J. H. Cooper	1947-48	T. S. Sharp
1917-18	J. H. Cooper	1948-49	F. E. Craze
1918-19	J. H. Cooper	1949-50	G. F. W. A. Bentley
1919-20	J. H. Cooper	1950-51	G. W. Cornelius
1920-21	J. S. Huggins	1951-52	E. A. Flemons (Mrs.)
1921-22	J. S. Huggins	1952-53	L. N. Hicks
1922-23	C. H. Bootyman	1953-54	A. J. Tremeer
1923-24	C. H. Bootyman	1954-55	A. B. Steart
1924-25	R. A. A. Jenkins	1955-56	E. M. Bishop
1925-26	R. A. A. Jenkins	1956-57	F. E. Martin
1926-27	R. A. A. Jenkins	1957-58	F. E. Craze
1927-28	R. A. A. Jenkins	1958-59	A. J. Tremeer
1928-29	R. A. A. Jenkins	1959-60	H. R. Denley
1929-30	R. A. A. Jenkins	1960-61	E. C. Mumford (Mrs.)
1930-31	A. H. Eggins	1961-62	J. H. Mumford
1931-32	A. H. Eggins	1962-63	J. H. Mumford
1932-33	G. H. K. Kingdon	1963-64	F. E. Martin
1933-34	G. H. K. Kingdon	1964-65	F. E. Martin
1934-35	J. S. Huggins	1965-66	K. G. M. Walke
1935-36	J. S. Huggins	1966-67	K. G. M. Walke
1936-37	G. W. H. Spanton	1967-68	J. C. P. Kingsland

TORBAY COUNTY BOROUGH COUNCIL
MAYORS FROM 1968/69 TO 1973/74

1968-69	A. L. Goodrich	1971-72	A. G. Illingworth
1969-70	F. W. H. Park	1972-73	F. E. Martin
1970-71	K. G. M. Walke	1973-74	D. G. Damerell

TORBAY BOROUGH COUNCIL
MAYORS FROM 1974/75 TO 1976/77

1974-75	H. S. Finch	1976-77	W. A. Beesley
1975-76	J. Farrell		

ᔕ PRESTON SANDS ᔔ

Preston Sands with the Redcliffe Hotel at the end of the Promenade, 1933.

An undeveloped Preston sea front in 1905. Paris Singer had plans to build several quality houses on the seaward side of the proposed marine drive but this never materialised. It was eventually left as an open space.

∾ PRESTON SANDS ∾

Shakespeare wrote – 'There is a tide in the affairs of men which if taken at the flood leads on to fortune'. However, on this occasion, not fortune, but a hasty retreat to Preston sea-front wall!!

Deckchairs throng the sea front at Preston Sands.

✧ PRESTON SANDS ✧

Left: *A mini view of Preston cliffs and rocks with a distant Torquay in the background.*

Right: *Preston North Sands looking towards Redcliffe Hotel.*

An onshore wind brings breakers to the busy Preston Sands in the 1950s.

≪ PRESTON CHURCH ≫

Right: *The temporary wooden church of St Pauls at Preston, which was demolished when the new permanent church was built.*

Below: *Preston's residential population has grown rapidly over the years and following the demolition of the previous wooden church, the new St Paul's was built.*

This photograph shows the laying of the foundation stone by the Lord Bishop of Exeter for the new church at Preston on 7 June, 1909.

CHAPTER 9

GOODRINGTON

The origin of the name Goodrington can be traced back to the Domesday Book, where it is recorded that Robert Marcelles, Knight, held the Manor of Godheringstone (1580–1640). In turn, this name originates from the Godheres people who were among the first settlers in South Devon.

In the 16th century Torbay was a highly favoured haven for fleets and warships of many nations which regularly visited the bay from the time of the Armada to the final defeat of Napoleon. It was common practice to unceremoniously dump ashore many sick or wounded seamen leaving them to die or become the responsibility of the local inhabitants. By 1693 this practice had led to an official complaint being made to the Treasury seeking compensation, for by this time there were, from the Grand Fleet alone, over 700 sick seamen being cared for in local private houses. It was not until the middle of the 18th century, however, that the Admiralty purchased three acres of land at Goodrington for use as a burial ground and there built a hospital with accommodation for a guard of soldiers. The situation became critical around 1797 when a flu epidemic raged rampant among warships in Torbay. One ship, the *Fortitude*, had to land 200 of her 600-strong crew in one night. Nearly 20 years later, in 1815, the Admiralty closed the hospital and the burial ground became sadly neglected.

The story of Goodrington's development to the resort which we know today began in 1921 when a scheme was approved to enhance the cliff facing Goodrington with a series of terraced walks and to prevent further shore erosion by building a strong retaining wall. Eight years passed before the Council were able to acquire the land which then happened to coincide with a national and international financial slump putting millions on the dole. With the advent of the Distressed Areas Relief Scheme, work commenced on the Goodrington Project in August 1929 with the arrival of a large contingent of unemployed Welsh miners. Soon the face of adjacent Roundham Head took on the appearance of a vast stone quarry. Despite bitter protests from local inhabitants, work proceeded to

plan with 80 000 tons of red rock being blasted away. By the winter of 1930–31, the protective sea wall and rock gardens were completed. It was at this time that Mr Herbert Whitley (owner of Paignton Zoo) generously donated hundreds of rare plants, shrubs and trees which were planted to beautify the terraced walks.

There now remained the vast area of swamp and wasteland, inland from the south and north sands, around which legend had spread that the swamp was bottomless and that on dark misty nights mysterious ghostly figures rose from its murky depths to carry off unwary travellers before returning to their subterranean dungeons at daybreak.

This myth was exploded in 1935 when the Council pressed on with what was described as a slum-clearance programme, the result of which was a beautiful laked park set out in verdant, floral and aquatic splendour, and in doing so discovered that the so-called bottomless marsh was only two feet deep!

The final phase of the development was the construction of a promenade across the south sands from Tanner's Lane to Cliff Park Lane. By the spring of 1936, the Goodrington scheme was complete with the builders having used 10 000 tons of concrete and provision made for 2½ miles of paths and walks.

This major undertaking was completed in May 1936 in the first year of the reign of King Edward VIII. After 325 days on the throne, however, the King abdicated and went by night from our shores to a foreign land and into exile. Almost exactly twelve months after the opening ceremony of the Goodrington reconstruction in May 1937, the Coronation of King George VI was celebrated.

Goodrington Sands and Goodrington Park now form one of the most attractive venues among the South West's coastal resorts. With the gentle sloping sands, nearby swan lake and model boat pond, the area has become a highly desirable destination for thousands of holiday visitors from all parts of the British Isles.

⊸ PICTURE POSTCARDS ⊸

This is a turn-of-the-century view of Preston Rocks showing Wheatridge Headland and in the distance, Torquay Harbour. Note the absence of hotels and private residences on the hills beyond.

The Pleasure Park at Goodrington had to wait many years before it was developed into what it is today. The expansion was not completed until 1936 at a cost of almost £55 000. This picture of Young's Park in the early 1920s shows cows grazing beside the lake.

PICTURE POSTCARDS

A comic card of a family bathing adventure in 1907.

Goodrington Sands at High Tide in 1912. These triangular Langford's tents were a novelty at the time but gave service as changing tents or beach huts. The sands were then known as a select retreat and could be reached by means of the ferry motor launch plying between Paignton, Goodrington and Torquay.

GOODRINGTON

An idyllic picture of Goodrington boating lake and its model-yacht pool in the late 1930s. The area overlooking the lakes has since been developed with hotels and private houses occupying the skyline.

Playtime among the pleasant shade of trees in the days when Goodrington Park was being developed in the very early 1930s.

∽ GOODRINGTON ∾

The car park and tea hut at the entrance to Goodrington Sands, c.1949. The car is probably an Austin 10 and to the right of the picture was a walk-through to the children's train ride circuit.

Goodrington North Sands before development began in 1929.

❧ GOODRINGTON ❧

The mammoth Goodrington development began in 1929 but was not complete until two years later.
When these two pictures were taken, the project had not started so it places the date at pre-1929.
The pictures show the cliff formation on the Roundham projection from which many tons of
red rock were quarried to build the protective sea wall and rock gardens.

GOODRINGTON

Early morning at Goodrington North Sands with the ebb tide revealing a magnificent stretch of sand from its low tidal limit to the flood (seaweed) line near the bathing huts. A turn-of-the-century photograph with the distant hills almost devoid of buildings.

Goodrington Sands, 1935. A fair number of people are bathing here on this sunny August afternoon. Because of the sun's rays on these shallow tidal sands, the temperature of the sea water sometimes reached as high as 67 degrees Fahrenheit.

GOODRINGTON

A rare view of Goodrington which takes in the cliffs at Roundham,
Young's Park and part of Goodrington Sands.

SUBSCRIBERS

Sheila Aspland, Paignton, Devon
Robert and Julie Bailey, Paignton, Devon
Harry and Jean Bartlett, Brixham, Devon
R. Bee, Paignton, Devon
Tony and Annette Bell, Paignton, Devon
Anne and John Bennett, Torquay, Devon
Paul F. Bevan, Paignton, Devon
Eric L. Bird, Paignton, Devon
C. Blake, Bradford-on-Avon, Wilts.
G. R. Blake, Churston, Devon
C. H. (Tim) Boddy, Paignton, Devon
L. Bowden, Paignton, Devon
Roger T. A. Bowden
Janet Y. P. Bray-Pullin
Mr D. A. Brooks, Paignton, Devon
Mr Paul J. Brown, Paignton, Devon
Russell and Sylvia Brown
Dave I. Browne, Paignton, Devon
Lesly E. E. Bruce-Watson, Paignton, Devon
Mrs Frances M. Brunt (née Pearse), Paignton, Devon
K. J. Burrow, Bucks Cross, Devon
Jacqui A. Carter, Perth, Western Australia
Joyce L. Caunter
John Christer, Churston, Brixham, Devon
J. W. Christer, Paignton, Devon
Peter Coetzee, Blagdon, Paignton, Devon
Steven Coldridge, Paignton, Devon
B. M. Cole, Paignton, Devon
Rex Coombe, Paignton, Devon
Terence Coombe, Paignton, Devon
Francis John Corner, Paignton, Devon
Peter James Cottam, Paignton, Devon
Charles R. Crewes, Brixham, Devon
Joyce and David Crimp, Paignton, Devon
Susan Dabbs (née Carley), Thornbury, Bristol
Mr and Mrs T. Davies, Fleet, Hampshire
Barbara Davies (née Edworthy), Brixham, Devon
Pauline and Dennis Day, Paignton, Devon
Arthur R. Day, Paignton, Devon
John Day, Brixham, Devon
Joe Dean, Paignton, Devon
W. H. W. Deller, Paignton, Devon
Dorothy Denner, Paignton, Devon
G. Diggines, Paignton, Devon
Anne S. Diggins
Mrs Sheila Drake (née Battershill), Paignton, Devon
Christopher N. Dransfield, Paignton, Devon

Michael and Joyce Dunne, The Seaspray Hotel, Paignton, Devon
A. C. Easterbrook, Paignton, Devon
Sheila M. Edwards, Paignton, Devon
George W. H. Ellis, Torquay, Devon
Cynthia L. and Joseph C. Evans, Paignton, Devon
Christine F. Farr, Paignton, Devon
Robert A. Finch, Paignton, Devon
Mr and Mrs J. Fleet, Paignton, Devon
Norman and Rosemary Frost, Newton Abbot, Devon
M. A. Gagg, Paignton, Devon
Eileen L. M. Galling, Weymouth, Dorset
Sheila M. Gannicott, Paignton, Devon
Michael William Nowell Garry, Paignton, Devon
William Robert George, Paignton, Devon
Peter N. H. Gibbs, Paignton, Devon
Alan C. G. Gibbs, Fulbourn, Cambridge
Margaret A. Glanville, Paignton, Devon
Mrs Doreen E. Glover, Paignton, Devon
Lesley Goillau, Paignton, Devon
Maureen Grant
Ben and Sam Griffin, Paignton, Devon
David Halfhide, Paignton, Devon
Kay Patricia Hammond, Broadstairs, Kent
Valerie D. Hammond, Paignton, Devon
Brian Harris, Paignton, Devon
Raymond S. Harvey, Paignton, Devon
David and Peggy Head, Paignton, Devon
Donald and Lorna Head, Epsom, Surrey
The Healey family, Paignton, Devon
Angela G. Herman, Paignton, Devon
Margaret H. Hewett, Paignton, Devon
Anthony Hill, Baldrine, Isle of Man
E. G. Hithersay, Paignton, Devon
Derek T. Holgate, Paignton, Devon
George Hopkins, Okehampton, Devon
Patricia M. Isaac, Paignton, Devon
Mr Peter E. J. Jeavons, Brixham, Devon
Shane L. Jeffery, Paignton, Devon
Rosie A. Jeffery, Paignton, Devon
Kevin and Nicola Jeffery, Paignton, Devon
Jason and Julie Jeffery, Paignton, Devon
Mrs Patricia M. Kemp, Paignton, Devon
R. and Y. Knapp, Paignton, Devon
Robert and Jean Knight, Paignton, Devon
B. Lane, Paignton, Devon
Mr P. H. Lee, Taunton, Somerset

Jean Lewis and Sally, Redstone, Paignton, Devon
Conway Longworth-Dames, Paignton, Devon
Barrie Luscombe, Paignton, Devon
Keith Marshall, Paignton, Devon
Diane Massey (née Warburton), Paignton, Devon
Reginald J. Maunder, Paignton, Devon
Mr Michael McElheron, Kingskerswell, Devon
Mr P. P. McElhinney, Paignton, Devon
Lois H. Middleton, Paignton, Devon
Brian Moore, Paignton, Devon
Eder P. E. Mosedale, Paignton, Devon
Tony Moss, Paignton, Devon
Janet Newby, Homebourne House, Paignton, Devon
Mr Michael P. Norsworthy, Paignton, Devon
Deborah Y. O'Donovan, Paignton, Devon
Peter J. Palmer, Paignton, Devon
Gillian Rose Parker, Paignton, Devon
Margaret and Denis Parkin and family, Paignton, Devon
Kenneth R. Parnell, Paignton, Devon
John G. Parnell, Bovey Tracey, Devon
Gordon and Stella Partridge, Goodrington, Devon
Bernard E. Pearce, Brixham, Devon
Ken Pearse, Paignton, Devon
Reginald A. L. Pearse, Paignton, Devon
Anne and John Pentney, Paignton, Devon
K. Penwill, Paignton, Devon
Jeanne E. Peters, Paignton, Devon
Graham and Andrea Platt, Paignton, Devon
Gwen Plows, Llancarfin, Wales
Joan I. Pook, Paignton, Devon
Tony L. Rayner, Paignton, Devon
Dennis and Myris Redgrave, Paignton, Devon
'Wag' and Joyce Rivers, The Devonport Arms, Paignton, Devon
Mr Michael W. Rodgers, Paignton, Devon
Tony Rogers, Paignton, Devon
W. Harold Rumbelow, Paignton, Devon
Sacred Heart RC Primary School, Paignton, Devon
Mr Mark A. Satchell, Paignton, Devon
Ilene Savill, Galmpton, Devonshire
Josephine M. Schofield, Broadsands, Paignton, Devon
Sharon and Tim Schofield, Paignton, Devon
Suzanne and David Schofield, Park Hotel, Paignton, Devon
A. F. Sherrell, Paignton, Devon
Frances E. Simpson, Paignton, Devon
George and Pearl Simpson, Paignton, Devon
Mr Derek and Mrs Wendy Smith, Marine Hotel, Paignton, Devon
Patricia Smith, Broadsands Park, Paignton, Devon
J. and N. Smythe, Paignton, Devon
V. F. and C. H. Spreadbury
Gerald L. Standlake, Paignton, Devon

Valerie Margaret Stephens, Paignton, Devon
Kay M. Sutton, Bere Alston, Devon
Avice V. Taft, Paignton, Devon
Mrs G. H. Taylor, Paignton, Devon
Mr and Mrs D. J. Teague, Paignton, Devon
John Brian and Sheila Thompson, Paignton, Devon
Jennifer and Graham Thorne, Maldon, Essex
Patrick J. Tobin, Paignton, Devon
Albert J. Tomlin, Paignton, Devon
The Torbay Bookshop, Torquay Road, Paignton
Torquay Central Library
Torre Abbey Historic House and Gallery, Torquay, Devon
Herbert J. Tozer, Paignton, Devon
Chris Trewern (née Whatman), Paignton, Devon
Harry C. Truscott, Paignton, Devon
Prebendary Brian Tubbs, The Vicarage, Paignton, Devon
Joseph Tucki, Colditzer, Paignton, Devon
Paul Vaggers, Paignton, Devon
A. Douglas Vaisey, Peterborough, Canada
Stephen Walker, Paignton, Devon
J. A. Wallace, Paignton, Devon
Raymond Waller, Paignton, Devon
John F. W. Walling, Newton Abbot, Devon
Roy and Eileen Ward, Brixham, Devon
Ken and Margaret Ward, Crowborough, East Sussex
Edward Ware, Paignton, Devon
E. A. Webber, Paignton, Devon
Shane N. and Paul J. Webber, Paignton, Devon
Dennis and Dorothy West, Paignton, Devon
Mrs Mollie E. P. Westlake (née Wills), Paignton, Devon
Michael Whatman, Paignton, Devon
Graham Wheatley, Paignton, Devon
Mrs Edna L. White, St Marychurch, Torquay, Devon
David Wield, Paignton, Devon
Jill Williams, Paignton, Devon
Brenda Williams, Paignton, Devon
Alan Wills, Paignton, Devon
Kenneth E. Wills, Paignton, Devon
Gloria and Arnold Wilson, Paignton, Devon
William E. Wood, Suffield, CT, USA
Mrs Sue Woodward, Paignton, Devon
Michael and Karen Woodwark, Fulham, London SW6
Patrick and Linda Woodwark, Paignton, Devon
Chris and Geraldine Woodwark, Dartmouth, Devon
Anthony and Janice Woodwark, Ipplepen, Devon
David and Elvin Wooldridge, Hotel Bonair, Paignton, Devon
Alexander D. Wooler, Paignton, Devon
Edward A. Woolvett, Paignton, Devon
Raymond John Yates, Paignton, Devon

ALSO AVAILABLE IN
THE SERIES

The Book of Addiscombe • Various
Book of Bampton • Caroline Seward
Book of Bickington • Stuart Hands
Blandford Forum: A Millennium Portrait • Various
The Book of Brixham • Frank Pearce
The Parish Book of Cerne Abbas • Vale & Vale
The Book of Chittlehampton • Various
The Book of Constantine • Moore & Trethowan
The Book of Cornwood and Lutton • Various
The Book of Creech St Michael • June Small
The Book of Cullompton • Various
The Book of Dawlish • Frank Pearce
The Ellacombe Book • Sydney R. Langmead
The Book of Grampound with Creed • Bane & Oliver
The Book of Hayling Island and Langstone • Rogers
The Book of Helston • Jenkin with Carter
The Book of Hemyock • Clist & Dracott
The Book of High Bickington • Avril Stone
The Book of Ilsington • Dick Wills
The Book of Lamerton • Ann Cole and Friends
Lanner, A Cornish Mining Parish • Scharron Schwartz & Roger Parker
The Book of Loddiswell • Various
The Book of Lustleigh • Joe Crowdy
The Book of Manaton • Various
The Book of Meavy • Pauline Hemery
The Book of Morchard Bishop • Jeff Kingaby
The Book of Minehead with Alcombe • Binding & Stevens
The Book of North Newton • Robins & Robins
The Book of Pimperne • Compiled by Jean Coull
The Book of Plymtree • Tony Eames
The Book of Porlock • Denis Corner
Postbridge – The Heart of Dartmoor • Reg Bellamy
The Book of Priddy • Various
The Book of Rattery • Various
The Book of Silverton • Various
The Book of South Stoke • Various
South Tawton and South Zeal with Sticklepath • Roy and Ursula Radford
*The Book of Sparkwell with Hemerdon
& Lee Mill* • Pam James
The Book of Stithians • Various
The Book of Swanage • Rodney Legg
The Book of Torbay • Frank Pearce
Uncle Tom Cobley and All: Widecombe-in-the-Moor • Stephen Woods
The Book of Watchet • Compiled by David Banks
The Book of West Huntspill • Various
Widecombe-in-the-Moor • Stephen Woods
The Book of Williton • Michael Williams
Woodbury: The Twentieth Century Revisited • Roger Stokes
The Book of Woolmer Green • Various

SOME OF THE MANY
FORTHCOMING TITLES

The Book of Addiscombe; Vol. II • Various
The Book of Barnstaple • Avril Stone
The Book of Bridestowe • R. Cann
The Book of Buckland Monochorum • Hemery
The Book of Carshalton • Stella Wilks
The Book of Chagford • Ian Rice
*The Book of Chittlehamholt with
Warkleigh & Satterleigh* • Richard Lethbridge
The Book of Colney Heath • Bryan Lilley
The Book of Culmstock • Robert Garrett
The Book of Down St Mary • Various
*The Book of Dulverton
with Brushford, Bury & Exebridge* • Various
The Book of Dunster • Hilary Binding
The Book of Exmouth • W.H. Pascoe
The Book of Leigh and Bransford • Various
The Book of Lulworth • Rodney Legg
The Book of Markyate • Richard Hogg
The Book of Mawnan Smith • Various
The Book of Newdigate • Various
The Book of Newton Abbot • Ian Rice
The Book of North Tawton • Various
The Book of Northlew with Ashbury • Various
The Book of Nynehead • Various
The Book of Okehampton • Roy and Ursula Radford
The Book of Peter Tavy • Various
The Book of Publow with Pensford • Various
*The Book of Sampford Courtenay
with Honeychurch* • Stephanie Pouya
The Book of Staverton • Pete Lavis
The Book of Studland • Rodney Legg
The Book of Whitchurch • Ann Pulford

For details of any of the above titles or if you are interested in writing your own community
history, please contact: Community Histories Editor, Halsgrove House, Lower Moor Way, Tiverton Business
Park, Tiverton, Devon EX16 6SS, England, e-mail:sales @halsgrove.com If you are particularly interested in
any of the images in this volume, it may be possible to supply a copy.
Please telephone 01884 243242 for details.

*In order to include as many historic photographs as
possible in this volume, a printed index is not
included. However, the Community Histories are
currently being indexed by Genuki. For further
information and indexes to volumes in the
series, please visit:
http://www.cs.ncl.ac.uk/genuki/DEV/indexingproject.html*